I0644066

AN ARCHAEOLOGICAL PORTRAIT OF LIFE IN A BRONZE AGE CYPRIOT VILLAGE

sidestonepress

AN ARCHAEOLOGICAL PORTRAIT OF LIFE IN A BRONZE AGE CYPRIOT VILLAGE

Scientific Explorations at Politiko-*Troullia*

STEVEN E. **FALCONER** AND PATRICIA L. **FALL**

Published by Sidestone Press, Leiden
www.sidestone.com
E-mail: info @ sidestone.nl
Phone: (+31)(0)71-7370131

Layout & cover design: Sidestone Press
Cover image: Drone photo of Politiko-*Troullia* and *Koliokremmos* by Elizabeth Ridder.

ISBN 978-94-6426-367-1 (softcover)
ISBN 978-94-6426-368-8 (hardcover)
ISBN 978-94-6426-369-5 (PDF e-book)

DOI: 10.59641/d4g0a1b2c3

Contents

In loving memory of

Bob Erskine, Ron Gardiner, Tom Davis, and Clark Casebolt.

Dearest of friends and brothers in the field.

Preface

This portrait of Bronze Age life in Cyprus is inspired by the support and encouragement of our friends and neighbours in Pera Orinis, who hosted the members of our archaeological project during our annual field research from 2004 to 2019. We have particularly appreciated the enthusiastic participation of the students, parents, and teachers from schools in Pera and Kampia who joined us for mornings of excavation and afternoon lab work during our excavation seasons at Politiko-*Troullia*. This book is our modest expression of reciprocation and thanks to the people of Cyprus on behalf of all the students and staff members from the United States, Cyprus, Australia, Canada, and Poland who have contributed to our project's fieldwork, and to the analysis and interpretation of the wide variety of evidence these explorations have produced.

We present our story from two vantage points. We offer a descriptive explanation of how our project unfolded step by step, beginning with a brief synopsis of how archaeology works and then working through our field explorations, laboratory analysis, results, and their interpretation. We also introduce a first-person narrative (*in italics) in which we describe our research as you might have experienced it as a first-time archaeological volunteer*. As you will discover, archaeology is a team endeavour, and anyone who is willing to rise early, work hard, rough it a bit, and get dusty on a regular basis can experience life as a field archaeologist! We hope you enjoy this account of our archaeological project in action, and how it has illuminated the lives of the Cypriot predecessors who lived in the distant past, in this case 4000 years ago!

I

How Archaeology Works

1.1 Welcome to Our Research Project!

It all started one morning as I read an online story about new archaeological discoveries on Cyprus. The directors of an archaeological project at a place called Politiko-Troullia were reporting the results of last spring's fieldwork, and mentioned they were accepting applications for new volunteers for this year's excavations. It all sounded intriguing, but I was not studying archaeology, and I had already submitted applications for jobs that would start at the end of the semester. On the other hand, the prospect of something really different, a new adventure, held the appeal of venturing into the unknown! But I wondered: what is archaeology, and what is it like to be an archaeologist? I was about to find out!

1.2 What is Archaeology?

How do we explore what it was like to live in Bronze Age Cyprus? The people of prehistory lived in a world without writing, so they left us no documents that describe their lives firsthand. To tell their story we must rely on archaeology as a scientific means to interpret the material remains that prehistoric people did leave behind. These remains range from individual artifacts to the ruins of ancient settlements, to evidence of human activities spread across expansive landscapes. We investigate all these aspects of the archaeological record not only through excavation of ancient settlements, but also by using a variety of increasingly innovative methods, including satellite imagery, aerial (often drone-based) reconnaissance, soil erosion modelling, subsurface sensing using ground penetrating radar,

Figure 1. Drone photo facing southwest toward the Troodos Mountains of Cyprus showing the ploughed fields in which the Bronze Age village of Politiko-*Troullia* is buried, the locations of our main areas of excavation in *Troullia* East, West, and North, and the terraced hill slopes of Politiko-*Koliokremmos*.

magnetometry and soil resistivity to locate buried features, stable isotope analysis of animal bones and plant fragments, and chemical analysis of pottery using X-ray fluorescence and residue analysis. These diverse field and lab methods generate data that elucidate a growing array of insights into ancient life, ranging from locating buried settlements to assessing how landscapes changed over time, inferring how cultivated crops and animal herds were managed on those landscapes, and identifying how pottery was traded between communities.

This book portrays Bronze Age village life based on our analyses of evidence from the archaeological site of Politiko-*Troullia*[1] and its surrounding hinterland (Figure 1). Archaeologists use the term "site" to refer to a location of past human habitation or activity. We excavate sites to recover detailed evidence of the lives of our predecessors, and we use a variety of increasingly complex methods to analyse the material remains that ancient people have left behind and to infer the behaviour of our distant ancestors. After all, the primary goal of archaeology is to use evidence from the past to illuminate the lives of people whose behaviour

1 Archaeological sites on Cyprus are given two-part names, beginning with the name of the nearest modern settlement followed by an italicized toponym (a place name often derived from a distinctive landmark or feature of the local topography). In this case, there are several archaeological sites in the vicinity of the modern village of Politiko. The Greek term *Troullia* pertains to the fields immediately south of the monastery of Agios Irakleidios.

we can no longer observe, whose life stories are undocumented historically, and which can be linked in some cases to modern populations.

My application was accepted! And here I am at Larnaca Airport looking for other project members and volunteers. I spot them quickly based the broad-brimmed hats and sturdy hiking boots all of us have been advised to bring, and the slightly bewildered looks on some faces that tell me that I'm not the only person who is uncertain of what to expect in the coming weeks. Our project directors Steve and Pat, along with other staff members, arrive in a couple of pick-up trucks and a van that we all squeeze into with our suitcases and backpacks, and off we go! After about a 30-minute drive north, we turn toward the foothills of the Troodos Mountains, winding our way through the towns of Ayia Varvara, Mathiatis, Analiontas, and Kampia, before arriving at our home village of Pera Orinis. Here narrow cobbled streets between closely packed stone and mudbrick houses lead us down into the heart of the village that will be our adopted home for the next six weeks. We disperse to our accommodations in three rented houses, all built originally in the 19th century with some modern updates like electricity and indoor plumbing. Indeed, as I would soon realize, repeated construction and reconstruction is an architectural theme that hearkens back to the most ancient farming communities on Cyprus! Now that I have been introduced to our historic village, I begin wondering how archaeologists comprehend time, especially when it extends back through millennia from recent history into the deep prehistoric past?

1.3 Charting Time Archaeologically

How do archaeologists determine the age of ancient settlements and archaeological evidence? Archaeologists often divide long stretches of time into more manageable archaeological periods, which are defined by groups of artifacts that share a similar style or technology across a region. This method creates "relative chronologies" with time periods based on sequences of archaeological evidence. Archaeologists often subdivide timespans into early, middle and late subperiods, and adapt them to local archaeological evidence. For example, the relative chronology for prehistoric Cyprus includes the Early, Middle and Late Bronze ages, which are also known as the Early, Middle and Late Cypriot periods. Correlations of archaeological evidence with dated historical or natural events are used to anchor these relative chronologies (and the more anchors, the better). Scientists also have developed methods to generate "absolute chronologies" from archaeological evidence.

Absolute dates are expressed numerically, most familiarly in years BC or AD, but increasingly denoted in years BCE (Before the Common Era; before AD 1) or CE (Common Era; AD 1 and thereafter). Arguably the most influential absolute dating method in archaeology is radiocarbon dating, which we use to date organic archaeological samples (i.e., plant or animals remains; today most often carbonized seeds from short-lived annual plants) from as far back as about 50,000 years ago (Taylor and Bar-Yosef 2014). Each radiocarbon age provides an estimate of the date at which a plant or animal died and stopped absorbing the radioactive isotope ^{14}C. Radiocarbon dates are expressed in years BP (Before Present). Radiocarbon BP dates can be converted to years BCE or years CE through radiocarbon calibration (Reimer 2022). Archaeologists use 1950 CE for the "present," since this date lies just before atomic weapons testing introduced large amounts of radioactive isotopes into the earth's atmosphere.

The chronological setting of this book lies in the Bronze Age, which on Cyprus stretches between about 2400 and 1000 BCE (Knapp 2013: table 2). This term "The Bronze Age" was introduced in the early 19th century by the Danish antiquarian C. J. Thomsen as one of three ages of successive tool technologies (the Stone, Bronze, and Iron ages) that he associated with the evolution of prehistoric human societies. Although archaeologists no longer simply correlate these periods with their namesake technologies, this three-part nomenclature continues to provide the traditional basis for European, Near Eastern, and Mediterranean prehistoric chronologies. In practice, the Bronze Age has come to refer not only to bronze metallurgy but more importantly to the development of early cities and civilizations. On Cyprus, the timing of the Early, Middle and Late Bronze ages differs from that of nearby mainland regions around the Eastern Mediterranean. As we shall see, the prelude to Cypriot Bronze Age civilization featured a lengthy and intriguing era of preurban society, which we will explore through our analysis of the evidence from Politiko-*Troullia*.

1.4 Exploring Early Civilization on Cyprus

Our first afternoon in Pera Orinis is filled with nervous excitement, meeting fellow volunteers, and sharing our expectations for the coming days. Our project members include about 20 of us, plus a variety of staff members. I share a bedroom with three roommates, and the foot of my bed extends into the living room of our house, so I hope our cozy accommodations will inspire everyone to keep up their sense of humour! I am happily making new friends and learning that just about every volunteer is new to archaeology, like me. Little do I realize that some of them will become friends for life! Later in the day, our project directors and staff discuss with us why we are doing fieldwork at Politiko-Troullia, and what insights on life in prehistoric Cyprus we hope to discover.

One big question that archaeologists ask is "how and why did ancient societies develop civilization?" This phenomenon involved numerous changes in the way people lived, based especially on increasing differences between individuals and between communities in wealth, social status, and political power. In general terms, we can think of this as a process in which household-based society added a new level of authorities, often residing in cities, who made decisions over the people living in subordinate towns and villages. So, in this regard early civilization marked the birth of bureaucracy. In exchange for social benefits like communal defence, agricultural management, food storage and distribution, early bureaucrats might, for example, levy taxes, conscript labour for public works or negotiate treaties. The rise of civilization is reflected archaeologically in a variety of ways, including the appearance of cities and the development of societies in which the roles of individual people became increasingly specialized and differentiated. Bronze Age societies around the Mediterranean included some of the world's earliest examples of this process, and interestingly they differ considerably in how, where, and when they occurred. For example, the ancient populations of the Levant (the lands along the eastern seaboard of the Mediterranean: modern Lebanon, coastal Syria, Israel, Palestine and western Jordan) started building fortified towns about 3500 BCE, at the beginning of the Levantine Early Bronze Age. The Levant is generally more arid than Cyprus, so these communities tended to be situated near water sources and inhabited by farming populations for whom access to water was crucially important. Bronze Age Levantine families lived in settlements of densely packed mudbrick buildings year-round for multiple generations, sometimes over centuries or even millennia. The gradual decomposition and repeated rebuilding of their mudbrick structures led to the formation of ruin mounds known in Arabic and Hebrew as "*tells*," which provide prominent and unmistakable archaeological landmarks on Middle Eastern landscapes.

Archaeological investigation of the lives of Bronze Age Cypriots is particularly intriguing based a variety of characteristics, many of which stand in contrast to those of their mainland contemporaries.[2] Although access to water sources would have been important in both Cyprus and the Levant, Bronze Age Cypriot settlements were not as numerous or densely populated, nor were they occupied for time spans rivalling the longest occupied cities in the Middle East.[3] Perhaps because they were less constrained by population pressure, Cypriot communities and the households within them tended to relocate periodically, rather than persisting in long-term locations. For all these reasons, Cyprus does not feature mounded *tell*-like archaeological sites. This is just one trait whereby Cyprus offers a distinct archaeological legacy, one that reflects the island's own unmistakable path toward cities and civilization. In fact, Cypriot prehistory reminds us of archaeology's remarkable ability both to imagine past ways of life very unlike our own as well as to discover aspects of daily living similar to those of today.

Excavations across the island reveal that the buildings in Bronze Age Cypriot towns and villages were commonly constructed with stone foundations capped by mudbrick upper walls, probably resembling the older traditional houses found in many Cypriot villages today. These ancient communities were composed of structures that varied considerably in size and architectural plan, and in their configuration within settlements, as families grew from generation to generation. They were accompanied by a wide range of material remains that archaeologists analyse and interpret to infer what ancient people did in the course of their daily lives. The families in these communities engaged in varying combinations of farming, herding, hunting, metallurgy and craft manufacturing (like spinning, weaving, pottery making). Archaeology provides ample evidence for some aspects of daily life. For example, larger non-portable artifacts (e.g., heavy ground stone basins and large ceramic storage jars) may mark intentional activity locations, while smaller objects may be deposited more widely and accidentally. Shards of broken pottery, which preserve well,

---

2 The social identities of the Bronze Age peoples of Cyprus remain tantalizingly elusive. The Amarna Letters (diplomatic correspondence dating between 1360 and 1332 BCE from the royal archive of the pharaoh Akhenaten at Amarna, Egypt) mention "Alašiya," which may refer to a specific town on Cyprus (a common candidate is ancient Enkomi) or to the island as a whole (Artzy et al. 1976; Goren et al. 1993). In either case, the Amarna Letters provide the earliest historical references to Cyprus among Eastern Mediterranean civilizations.

3 For example, the Palestinian city of Jericho was founded about 9000 BCE (Gates 2003: 18), while Aleppo, Syria and Byblos, Lebanon have been inhabited continuously since about 5000 BCE (Mansel 2016: 15; Dumper et al. 2006: 104). The leading candidate for the longest continuously occupied settlement on Cyprus is Larnaca (ancient Kition), which was one of several Late Bronze Age cities founded about 1400 BCE (Knapp 2013: 352-355).

provide abundant remnants of ceramic vessels used for storage, cooking and serving of both liquids (like olive oil and wine) and dry commodities (such as grains or dried fruit). Likewise, bones from butchered animals provide direct evidence of animal management, including herding, hunting, butchering, and meat consumption. Other behaviours, however, have left us much less direct material evidence. Spinning and weaving are reflected indirectly by discarded spindle whorls and loom weights, rather than by textile products themselves, which rarely are preserved in open air sites like *Troullia* (but may be recovered from dry caves). Other important crafts, such as wood working and basketry, remain largely conjectural, as a result of the rapid decay of wood and natural fibres, and the challenge of identifying woodworking or basket weaving tools. Metal tools and weapons may have been discarded when they broke or wore out, or were subsequently re-smelted, thereby transforming these artifacts, delaying their discard, and minimizing the likelihood of their recovery. Thus, archaeologists reconstruct past ways of life from multiple lines of highly fragmentary material evidence that vary in abundance, degree of preservation, and connection to specific human activities.

This book explores the lives of Bronze Age Cypriots based on archaeological evidence from the ancient settlement of Politiko-*Troullia* and its surrounding landscape, which we have investigated and interpreted through survey, excavation, remote sensing, computer modelling and scientific analysis. Our investigations have generated multiple lines of inference that illuminate the lives of Politiko-*Troullia*'s inhabitants, which featured their cultivation of surrounding fields and orchards, herding and hunting of local animals, copper metallurgy, and communal social celebrations.

1.5 Scientific Study of Cypriot Bronze Age Society

As dusk approaches, our directors take us for an introductory visit to the site of Politiko-Troullia. Its fields are covered in dense stands of barley awaiting harvest. Our directors assure us that last year's fieldwork generated clear evidence that a Bronze Age settlement lies buried in these agricultural fields, but that conclusion certainly is not apparent to me. So, I ask our directors: "Why did you decide to work on the Bronze Age, and how did you decide to work at Politiko-Troullia, of all places?"

Archaeologists, like all scientists, propose ideas and explanations that are constantly discussed, critiqued, and changed with the arrival of new

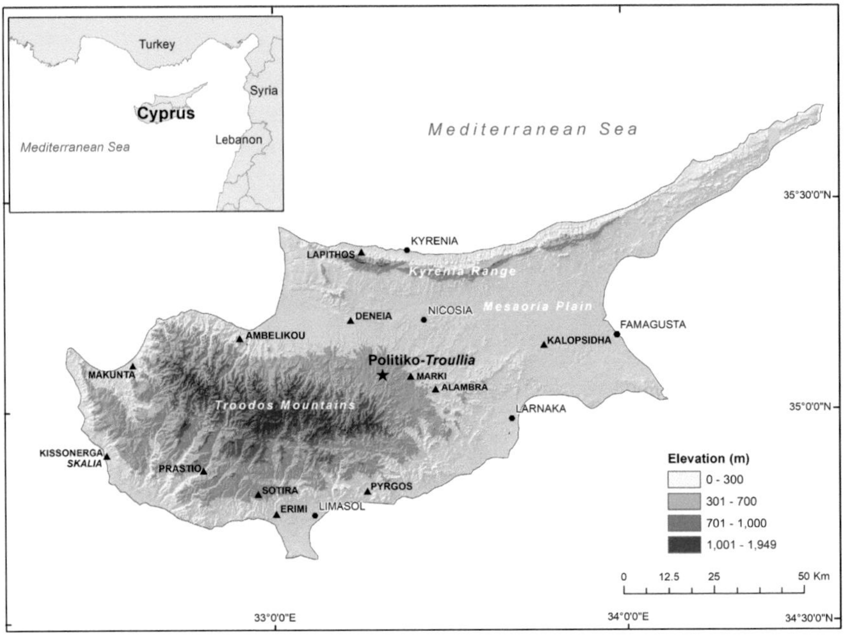

Figure 2. Relief map showing the location of Politiko-*Troullia* in the Troodos foothills, a variety of other excavated Bronze Age sites across the island (triangles), and modern cities of Cyprus (circles).

scientific methods, data, and interpretive ideas. We always start a project with challenges we want to address and questions we hope to answer. An archaeologist never just digs to see what they can find! We work from empirical data, which are based on the description, measurement and quantification of all the material evidence, no matter how fragmentary, that we recover using an increasingly wide variety of field and analytical methods. Since archaeologists often are confronted with unexpected evidence, we also necessarily maintain sufficient flexibility to adapt and revise our research questions and methods over the course of our field and laboratory investigations. Indeed, science is most intriguing when new insights or unexpected results inspire us to change our ideas, which makes scientific exploration exciting because its frontiers are constantly expanding. This process thrives by allowing room for new ideas, often presented as hypotheses, which can be thought of as scientifically testable propositions. As part of the archaeological explanation for the development of Cypriot civilization, one point of consensus is that the first cities of Cyprus, and their participation in trade across the Eastern Mediterranean, were established during the Late Bronze Age by about 1650 BCE (Knapp 2013; Manning 2013). Lively debate, based on evidence from a wide array of Bronze Age sites (Figure 2) currently leads to intriguingly different hypotheses for the nature of Cypriot communities and the lives of their inhabitants during the prelude to urbanism over the preceding two thousand years.

Most settlements during the Early and Middle Bronze Ages on Cyprus were dispersed, and most likely relatively autonomous, largely egalitarian agricultural communities (Crewe 2017). In archaeological terms, the members of "egalitarian" societies enjoyed similar access to wealth, social status, and political power (Andreou 2019). Interestingly, some Cypriot communities may have resisted unequal accumulation of material wealth and social status, thereby perpetuating relatively egalitarian living conditions during this lengthy prelude to the first cities (Peltenburg 1993). This possibility marks an intriguingly counterintuitive instance of a social "levelling" strategy that would be unusual and perhaps perceived as maladaptive in today's competitive urbanized world. It has been hypothesized further (Andreou 2019) that many small communities built cooperative social and economic networks across the island in the Middle Bronze Age. Their interaction was intensified in the Late Bronze Age in response to expanded international diplomacy and maritime trade in wine, olive oil, timber, and especially copper (Manning 2019; Webb and Knapp 2021), thereby providing the economic foundation for the establishment of Cypriot cities. These insights highlight the theoretical backdrop for our analysis of Politiko-*Troullia* as it illustrates life during the centuries leading to the island's first cities and urbanized society.

II

Field Investigations at Politiko-*Troullia*

2.1 Fieldwork Begins!

Between continued late-night banter with my roommates and the prospect of my first day of fieldwork, I slept little my first night. Even though we had been alerted that everyone should be ready to leave for the site before dawn, at 5:30am sharp, I am startled by my roommate shaking me to semi-consciousness in the faint early morning light. I glance bleary-eyed at my watch, which shows 5:13am, a time I hope is somehow simply a technical malfunction. But it isn't! I have slept through my alarm! I hurriedly pull on my light-weight pants, long-sleeve shirt, hiking boots, and broad-brimmed hat, all for protection against the sun and the rough terrain of the site. After grabbing a water bottle, slapping on sunscreen, and rummaging in my bag for my sunglasses, I gulp down a very quick cup of tea and munch on a digestive biscuit. In the ensuing days, a quick snack like this, maybe improved with a piece of toast and jam, comes to be known as "first breakfast." With this hasty preparation, I climb into one of the project vehicles for the five-minute ride from Pera to Politiko-Troullia. Fortunately, the project staff members have already packed our pick-up with tools, supplies, food and water: all the paraphernalia we will need for our first day's work.

Since beginning fieldwork on Cyprus in 2004, our project's mission has been to elucidate the daily life of a Cypriot community during the lead up to the island's first cities and civilization. The process of choosing a research locale began with a review of data from archaeological surveys conducted previously in the foothills of the Troodos Mountains (Given and Knapp 2003). These surveys identified several locales with abundant remains that hinted at Bronze Age settlements, particularly in the archaeologically rich landscape around the modern village of Politiko. In consultation with the Department of Antiquities of Cyprus, we proposed investigation of four sites and obtained a permit to begin fieldwork. Our initial reconnaissance showed that Politiko-*Troullia* was the most promising of these sites, with fields covered by ground stone artifacts and Red Polished Ware potshards, which are attributed to the Early and Middle Bronze ages. In addition, downcutting by adjacent Kamaras Creek had exposed archaeological deposits up to 3.5 metres deep (Falconer et al. 2005). We verified the archaeological depth of Politiko-*Troullia* by identifying nine locations where creek erosion had exposed buried stone walls. We used trowels to trim a vertical cross-section exposing one of these deep walls and several earthen floors next to it. During this trimming, we carefully collected potshards, fragments of sharp stone blades, animal bones, and plant remains from each of the archaeological layers we exposed. As a result of this initial fieldwork, we had our first clear look at Politiko-*Troullia*'s deeply stratified archaeological record.[4] All our initial results pointed to rich evidence from the Early and Middle Bronze Ages, making Politiko-*Troullia* particularly well suited for us to explore life in a Cypriot community during the prelude to urbanized civilization.

2.2 Archaeological Survey

After arriving in Pera, the staff assign everyone their responsibilities for the week. These range from daily housekeeping and kitchen duties (posted on the "dreaded" weekly chore list) to specific field and lab activities. For the first week, I am included in a group of four people to conduct an archaeological foot survey in search of clues to what lies buried beneath

4 "Stratification" refers to the layering of cultural sediments ("strata") that make up archaeological sites. Archaeologists conduct stratigraphic analysis of the ordering of these layers using, for example, the Principle of Superposition. This principle holds that in stratified sediments, the oldest layer is at the base and the layers ascending above it are progressively younger.

our feet. We use compasses to walk straight line transects across Politiko-Troullia, collecting surface artifacts (mostly potshards) in two-metre radius circles every 20 metres along our transects. With my nose to the ground, I carefully bag all the artifacts from each collection circle, write up a small tag identifying each circle's location, date of collection, and the names of our survey crew. Periodically, a field supervisor checks on our progress and reviews our collections with us. Even though they are covered with dust, most of our potshards have a shiny polished red finish. We quickly learn that this Red Polished Ware pottery dates primarily to the Middle Bronze Age. At 9am our project fieldwork manager calls out for everyone to take a break for "second breakfast!" Under the shade of an olive tree, we spread mats for a picnic feast of boiled eggs, cheese, olives, tomatoes, cucumbers, and oranges, and an array of other meze-style dishes that changes from day to day. This welcome interlude, with its excited chatter among the field crew, quickly becomes my favourite meal of the day!

The survey component of our project was designed with three main goals: 1) to determine the extent of archaeological remains at Politiko-*Troullia* and on the adjoining hill of Politiko-*Koliokremmos*, 2) to identify the major periods of ancient activity here, and 3) to locate concentrations of evidence to specify where people lived. Our survey collections documented potshards and ground stone artifacts spread over the entire 20-hectare expanse of *Troullia* and *Koliokremmos*,[5] and several concentrations of Red Polished Ware ceramics suggested the Middle Bronze Age village as the primary era of habitation (Falconer et al. 2005; Fall et al. 2012). In conjunction with our previous discoveries of eroded stone walls and deep archaeological sediments, our survey clearly indicated focal points of activity within a sizeable Bronze Age settlement that lay buried under the fields of Politiko-*Troullia*!

Our exploration also revealed numerous multi-course walls traversing the adjacent slopes of Politiko-*Koliokremmos* that were made from blocks of limestone bedrock and rounded igneous river cobbles. These walls still retain soil in an array of small arable fields that in antiquity would have augmented the croplands and pastures immediately surrounding the settlement at Politiko-*Troullia* (see Figure 1). This kind of agricultural terracing was a major aspect of ancient land management in this locality (Ridder et al. 2017) and elsewhere on Cyprus (Krahtopoulou

5 One hectare equals 10,000 square metres or about 2.47 acres.

and Frederick 2008; Bevan and Conolly 2011). Likewise, widespread potshards and fragments of ground stone vessels across Politiko-*Koliokremmos* strongly suggest that agricultural tasks were conducted on these hill slopes just beyond the settlement at *Troullia* and raise the distinct possibility that many of the terraces still visible on *Koliokremmos* were constructed originally in the Bronze Age (Fall et al., 2012; Galletti et al. 2013; Ridder et al. 2017). With these survey results in hand, we could start to envision the settlement and its surrounding landscape in time and space. The next step was to plan where and how to continue our investigations, especially our excavation of the buried village of Politiko-*Troullia*.

2.3 Soil Resistivity Testing

Following a few days of pedestrian survey, I am assigned to help one of our project surveyors conduct soil resistivity testing to locate the stone foundations of the Bronze Age buildings that are buried below the modern surface of Troullia. Each morning over the course of this week I help ready our soil resistivity equipment by attaching a battery pack and data recorder to a hand-held frame with two long metal probes (Figure 3). This instrument sends a mild electrical current from one pole to the other and measures the electrical resistance between the poles. Higher resistance values (measured in ohms) suggest that the electrical current is impeded by a buried object, and linear patterns of higher resistance strongly imply buried stone walls. Soil resistivity testing, which seemed simple to me at first blush, proved to require meticulous concentration and serious perseverance. Following the transects across Politiko-Troullia used for pedestrian survey, we laid out 20x20 metre grids in which we measured and recorded individual resistance readings at one-metre intervals. This meant that each grid required 400 individual readings!

Our project members conducted soil resistivity survey in 26 of these grids. Through careful teamwork and lots of double-checking, we ultimately recorded and mapped 10,400 readings over more than one full hectare, or roughly half of the area in which we expected the remains of Politiko-*Troullia* to be buried! By reviewing the results of our soil resistivity testing at the end of each day, we determined the most promising locations for unearthing the settlement beneath the modern fields of Politiko-*Troullia*. Two areas with readily apparent rectangular configurations of buried walls were designated “*Troullia* East”

Figure 3. Soil resistivity survey in the fields of Politiko-*Troullia*, with the church of Agios Irakleidios in the background, photo facing north.

Figure 4. Image from the Quickbird satellite overlaid with the four fields of our investigations at Politiko-*Troullia* and Politiko-*Koliokremmos*. Excavation units in yellow, agricultural terraces on Politiko-*Koloikremmos*, and vegetation indicated in red. Image with north at the top. Excavation units of *Troullia* North (4 units) and *Troullia* West (17 units) in Field 1, seven units of *Troullia* East in Field 2, plus single units spread across Fields 2, 3, and 4. The Pediaios River floodplain and Kamaras Creek bound Politiko-*Troullia* and Politiko-*Koliokremmos* on the east and west respectively; both watercourses flow south to north.

(northwest corner of Field 2) and "*Troullia* North" (northern end of Field 1) and a network of intersecting wall alignments along Kamaras Creek was labelled "*Troullia* West" (large excavation area along western edge of Field 1) (Figure 4). With this strategically important information in hand, we implemented a strategy for excavating Politiko-*Troullia* and reconstructing the activities of its inhabitants.

Figure 5. A grid of multiple adjacent excavation units in *Troullia* West being excavated under sunshades, with the incised ravine of Kamaras Creek in the left foreground. Note excavated sediment being sieved and growing piles of sifted back dirt, photo facing northeast.

2.4 Excavation of Politiko-*Troullia*

Now that we are ready to begin excavating, our project is settling into a regular daily routine. The members of our field crew are becoming increasingly accustomed to and appreciative of our pre-dawn wake up (some more than others!). I realize now that our lengthy daily schedule is all about maximizing our use of daylight and minimizing the effects of the midday heat. As our field season progresses, I shift from pulling on a jumper in the morning for a bit of warmth, to wearing the lightest, loosest fitting clothing I have, and covering my face and hands with lots of sunscreen! Shade becomes ever more precious for second breakfast, our field supervisors remind us to drink lots of water, and we make a point of finishing each day's fieldwork by 1pm, before the day reaches its peak temperature. Now that we are shifting to excavation, I soon discover that archaeologists are very systematic in determining where and how they dig!

Figure 6. The authors using trowels to reveal a Bronze Age earthen floor and the top of a stone wall in Politiko-*Troullia* East, photo facing northwest.

Archaeologists carefully plan the size, shape, and number of units in which they excavate. When ruins are visible across a modern landscape, excavation units can be aligned to architectural remains. Excavation of buried settlements, however, generally entails square or rectangular units whose placement is guided by preliminary investigations using satellite imagery, pedestrian survey, and subsurface testing (like soil resistivity). Following common practice at Bronze Age settlements in the Eastern Mediterranean and Middle East, we excavated in 4x4 metre squares. Within each unit we plotted the precise locations of walls, features like storage pits, and even individual artifacts. We investigated larger expanses using a grid of multiple contiguous excavation units (Figure 5) separated by walls of unexcavated sediment one metre wide, referred to as "baulks." Whatever the size of their units, archaeologists are meticulous in trimming their side walls vertically and drawing the stratified archaeological layers their excavations have revealed. Most archaeological "digging" recovers material evidence by systematic loosening sediments with hand pics and careful scrapping with a flat-bladed mason's trowel (Figure 6). At Politiko-*Troullia*, all the sediments we excavated were then sieved through 0.5x0.5 centimetre metal mesh (Figure 7) to comprehensively recover material evidence of Bronze Age life ranging from broken potshards and discarded fragments of animal bones to inadvertently lost personal items like carved stone beads or copper sewing needles. Our stratigraphic drawings also provide us with a record of the sediments we have removed, enabling us to reconstruct the chronological sequence in which these strata and their material remains were deposited.

I am assigned to an excavation unit in Troullia West, along with a unit supervisor and two other volunteers who will be my compatriots in the dirt during the coming weeks. I quickly realize that I had a preconceived notion (perhaps from watching archaeology documentaries on TV) that much of our work would involve detailed recovery of sparse individual artifacts with very small tools (I even brought a set of dental picks given to me by my enthusiastic family dentist). Instead, we start digging our unit with large picks and farming hoes to loosen the soil, followed by flat-bladed mason's trowels and metal dustpans, which we use to scoop this soil into buckets. And amid all our excavated sediment, we start finding myriad remains left by the ancient occupants of Politiko-Troullia! We devote great attention to using our trowels to scrape our unit in relatively flat levels, followed by sweeping up our loose dirt into plastic buckets so that we

Figure 7. Excavation of archaeological sediments in Politiko-*Troullia* East with a hand pick, showing the north slope of Politiko-*Koliokremmos* in the background. All excavated sediments were sieved through 0.5x0.5 centimetre metal mesh (as shown here) to recover artifacts and ecofacts, photo facing southeast.

Phase	West	North	East	Time Span BCE
1a	X			1930~1900
1b	X	X	X	1960-1930
2	X	X		1980-1960
3	X			2000-1980
4	X			2020-2000
5	X			2050-2020

Table 1. Stratigraphic phases in each of the areas excavated (West, North & East) at Politiko-*Troullia*. Time spans based on statistical modelling of 25 radiocarbon dates (Falconer et al. 2023).

can clearly see what we are uncovering and exactly where any exposed remains lie. Likewise, we make a special point of compulsively trowelling the side walls of our unit vertically, so that we can keep track of each layer of sediment we excavate. All this scraping and sweeping to keep the archaeological sediments in our unit "clean" is certainly out of the ordinary, but the importance of this weird tidiness becomes increasingly clear to me, and I soon realize that my trowel is my most important and versatile friend in this endeavour! Through our carefully controlled digging, we soon corroborate the results of our soil resistivity testing, in intriguingly different ways across the site!

Our excavations revealed that the buildings of Politiko-*Troullia* were constructed and reconstructed in a sequence of six stratified phases (labelled Phases 5, 4, 3, 2, 1b, and 1a, from earliest to latest). The remains of each phase are layered above those of the preceding phase and below those of the subsequent phase. In *Troullia* West we exposed evidence from all six phases, covering the timespan from the founding of Politiko-*Troullia* at the beginning of Phase 5 to its abandonment at the end of Phase 1a (Table 1). *Troullia* North provides evidence from Phases 2 and 1b, while *Troullia* East represents a single episode of habitation during Phase 1b. The varying combinations of phases in different parts of Politiko-*Troullia* reflect the tendency of prehistoric Cypriot communities to periodically relocate or remodel portions of their settlement, thereby creating a complicated overlay of occupied, reconfigured, and vacated structures through time.

2.4.1 Radiocarbon Dating of Politiko-*Troullia*

Our reconstruction of the history of Politiko-*Troullia* is founded on the settlement's six-phase stratigraphic sequence. Comparison of our pottery with descriptions, drawings, and photographs of ceramics from other excavations on Cyprius initially suggested habitation during the Early and Middle Bronze Ages (Fall et al. 2008). We subsequently refined our chronology through radiocarbon analysis of 25 seed and charcoal samples that we recovered from sediments in all six phases at Politiko-*Troullia* (Falconer et al. 2023). Mathematical modelling of our radiocarbon ages[6] has enabled us to estimate the absolute dates for the beginning and end of each phase, providing a much more specific timeline for the

6 We conducted Bayesian probabilistic modelling using "Oxcal," an online program for analysing stratified sequences of radiocarbon dates (https://c14.arch.ox.ac.uk/oxcal.html).

Figure 8. Project staff members and students from Pera Orinis celebrate a morning of excavation at Politiko-*Troullia* in 2011, photo facing north.

occupation of Politiko-*Troullia* between about 2050 and 1900 BCE. Our absolute radiocarbon chronology shows that each phase lasted only about 20-30 years, or roughly the timespan of one generation (based on the length of human generations in prehistory; Wang et al. 2023). In other words, village buildings tended to last only about one generation before they were reconstructed, demolished or abandoned.

During every workday I chat with the staff supervisor for my excavation unit, who fills their field notebook with a description of the day's excavation progress, a scale drawing showing where we have dug, and numbered lists of all the evidence we have found. It seems to me that we can think of an archaeological excavation as a giant three-dimensional jigsaw puzzle. As archaeologists, we define all the puzzle pieces, determine how they fit together, and use the reassembled puzzle to explore the Bronze Age life story of Politiko-Troullia. But no matter how intriguing, our work is somewhat less than glamorous! After all, most archaeological remains represent ancient refuse that was intentionally or unintentionally discarded. It is our job as excavators to recover as many of these remains as possible, and to document their context (i.e., exactly where we recovered them). As we dig, we inevitably become covered in dust as we loosen the earth with our picks and hoes, and shovel our dirt into plastic buckets. Now comes the really dusty part: we carry our buckets of dig dirt to a standing sieve and pour it onto a 0.5x0.5 cm mesh screen. With some hearty shaking, our dirt gradually disintegrates, leaving behind the archaeological remains that provide our basic data, and generating massive clouds of dust that leave us all cloaked in a pale brown hue that matches the fields of Politiko-Troullia! As a special treat, each season our project invites local school children, their teachers and parents to join us for a day of excavation (Figure 8), *which provides a particularly engaging hands-on experience with the tangible evidence of Cypriot prehistory for our friends and neighbours.*

2.4.2 The Bronze Age Settlement Emerges

As the remains of 4000-year-old village structures emerged from our excavations more and more clearly, we swept them thoroughly in preparation for photography and for stone-by-stone drawings. Each resulting plan view provides an effective tool for differentiating the architecturally defined interior and exterior spaces (which we termed "sectors") in which the occupants of Politiko-*Troullia* performed their daily activities and participated in special events through the course of their lives. The excavation of *Troullia* East uncovered stone walls that aligned precisely where our soil resistivity survey predicted. These walls defined a compound with a two-room house surrounded by smaller outbuildings and workspaces (Figure 9). The remains of *Troullia* East revealed three roofed rooms (Figure 10, sectors 1, 2, and 5) marked by substantial stone foundations bounding clearly defined interiors, with a stone door socket at the entrance to Sector 1 on which a door swung open and closed. A large storage bin (Sector 3) just outside this front door contained abundant shards from large storage jars. An adjacent covered courtyard (Sector 6) served as an exterior workspace for copper metallurgy (based on evidence we discuss below). Small enclosures (including Sector 4) lay to the north, while the external space just south of these buildings (Sector 7) was nearly devoid of material remains, suggesting that this compound may have been separated from other village structures by open space. In *Troullia* North our excavations exposed another compound centred on a square building featuring the remains of a domed terra cotta oven (Figure 11) possibly like the traditional ovens still found in the courtyards of many Cypriot homes today.

Figure 9. Stone wall foundations of a multi-room compound excavated in Politiko-*Troullia* East. Room interior with pit for roof support pillar to the right, exterior metallurgical workspace being swept at centre rear, and outbuildings in the foreground and to the left, photo facing southeast.

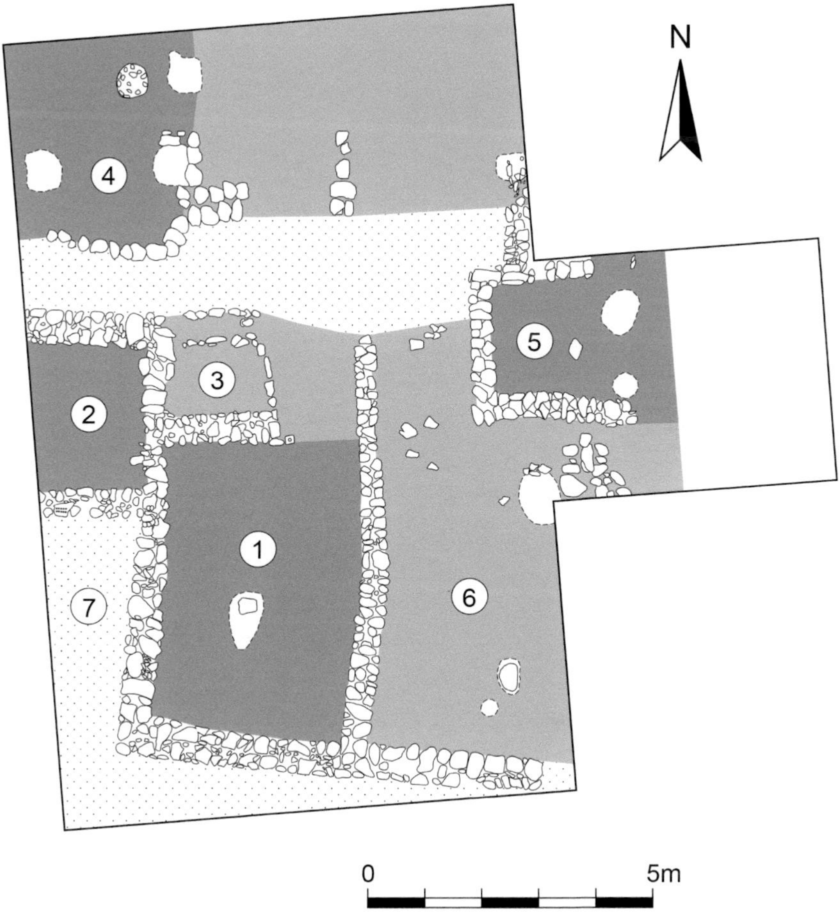

Figure 10. Plan view of stone walls revealed by excavation of Politiko-*Troullia* East, including numbered architectural spaces or "sectors." Solid lines indicate stones; dashed lines show pits, plus a posthole in Sector 1 and a metallurgical pit furnace at the northeast corner of Sector 6. Note square stone door socket on the west side of the entry to Sector 1.

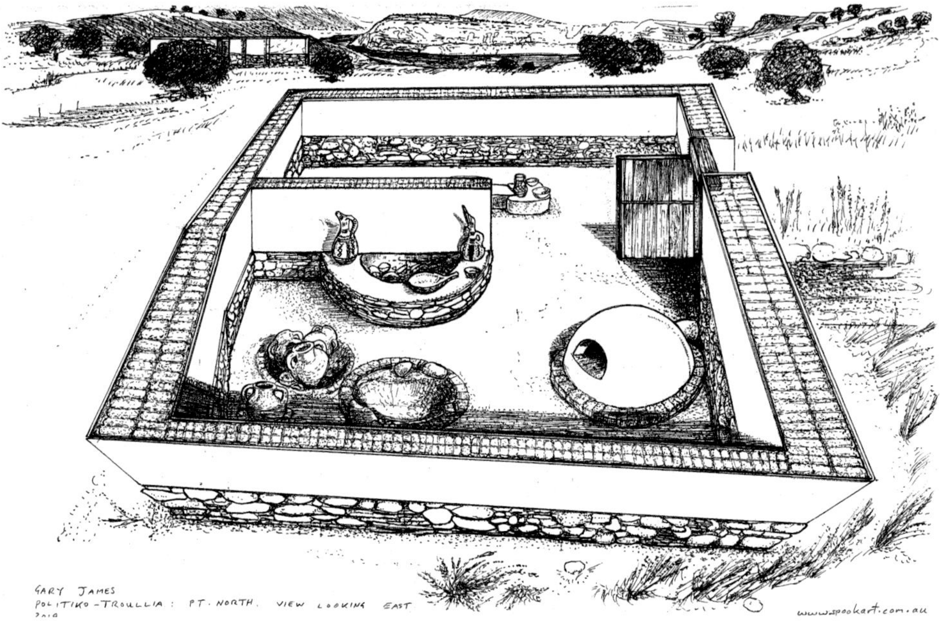

Figure 11. Artistic depiction of two-roomed structure in Politiko-*Troullia* North bult with stone foundations and mudbrick walls. Roof omitted to show terra cotta oven and stone-lined pits, facing east; structures of *Troullia* East in background at left (drawing by Gary James).

Guided by the soil resistivity alignments in *Troullia* West, our excavations revealed a particularly extensive network of numerous stone walls, including an intriguing surprise. During the Medieval Period, local workmen dug a trench down into a Bronze Age wall where they buried a terra cotta pipeline that brought water from a spring south of Politiko-*Troullia* downslope to Agios Irakleidios Monastery (Figure 12). We determined that this pipeline was laid sometime between the 12th and 15th centuries CE, based on a shard of glazed Sgraffito Ware pottery dating to the Lusignan Dynasty, which we found directly under a section of pipe (Falconer et al. 2012). Today, modern plastic piping continues to supply water to the monastery.

Over several excavation seasons, we expanded our grid of excavation units in *Troullia* West to expose an array of buildings, large courtyards, and an alley along the eastern bank of Kamaras Creek (Figure 13). The Bronze Age structures in *Troullia* West span the entire history of this

Figure 12. Excavation reveals a medieval terra cotta pipeline dug into Bronze Age stone walls in Politiko-*Troullia* West, photo facing north.

Figure 13. The Southern Courtyard excavated in Politiko-*Troullia* West (with embedded gaming stone toward the far end of the courtyard) and alleyway in foreground that led down to the waters of Kamaras Creek to the left, photo facing northwest.

village, from founding to abandonment, and feature two large, open courtyards (the Northern and Southern Courtyards; Sectors 8 and 9, respectively) and an alley (Sector 13) that sloped down to Kamaras Creek from east to west (Figure 14). The rooms forming sectors 10, 11, and 12 have been truncated by major downcutting along Kamaras Creek, while Sector 14 was open space with very few archaeological remains, possibly marking the southern edge of the village. Our excavations in *Troullia* West recovered particularly informative evidence of everyday life based on voluminous household trash discarded in its alleyway and striking evidence of communal activities reflected in the remains of feasting, spinning, weaving, and socializing found in the Southern Courtyard. Thus, the stratigraphic sequence and spatial patterning of archaeological remains at Politiko-*Troullia* allow us to discern the life history of this community, including the differing activities of its inhabitants over about 5-7 generations, between its original founding around 2050 BCE and its eventual abandonment after about 1900 BCE.

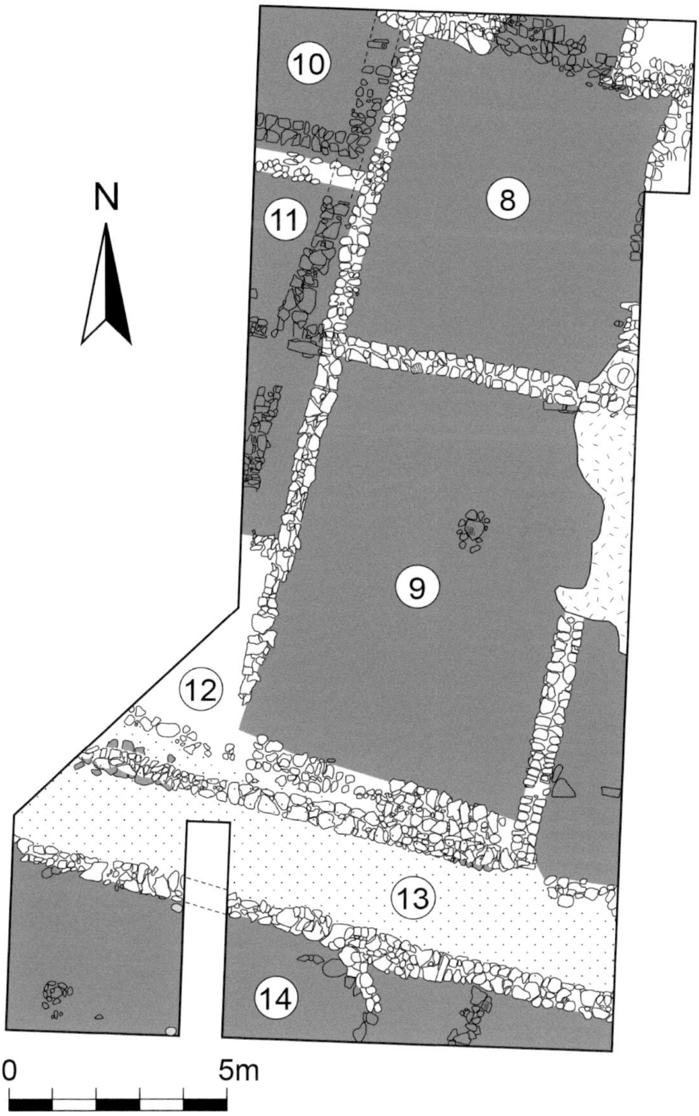

Figure 14. Plan view of stone walls revealed by excavation of Politiko-*Troullia* West. Darker stones indicate walls dating to Phases 4 and 3; lighter stones date to Phases 2 and 1. The hatched area indicates exposed bedrock cut back to form the northeast corner of the Southern Courtyard (Sector 9). Note the gaming stone embedded in the floor of the Southern Courtyard in Phases 4 and 3.

III

Deciphering Archaeological Evidence

With the analogy of a 3-D jigsaw puzzle in mind, the most basic pieces of archaeological puzzles include "artifacts" (anything made or modified by people) and "ecofacts" (remains of plants and animals used by people). The fundamental scientific mission of archaeologists is to identify, analyse and interpret the patterning of artifacts and ecofacts, so that we can infer how people lived their lives in the past. The village of Pera kindly made their historic 19th century girl's schoolhouse available for laboratory space where we conducted our initial analysis of all the artifacts and ecofacts recovered from our survey and excavations. As we shall see, the archaeological puzzle of Politiko-*Troullia* reveals a variety of household activities and craft industries that were vital to this community, featuring striking evidence of copper metallurgy in *Troullia* East and North, as well as spinning, weaving, dyeing and communal social events in *Troullia* West!

3.1 Artifacts: The Objects People Make and Use

3.1.1 Pottery

The most abundant artifacts at Politiko-*Troullia*, and at virtually all Bronze Age archaeological sites on Cyprus, are potshards, fragments of broken pottery. During the Early and Middle Bronze Ages, Cypriot potters crafted their ceramics by hand, at a time when artisans were introducing the fast kick wheel for making pottery in the Levant and Mesopotamia (Baldi

Figure 15. Two-handled ceramic cooking pot reconstructed from shards excavated at Politiko-*Troullia* West.

and Roux 2016). Cypriot household vessels included large jars for storing dry and liquid commodities, ovoid pots for cooking meals (Figure 15), and bowls in a range of sizes for serving individuals or groups of people (Figure 16). While kick wheel production encouraged mass production of increasingly standardized pottery in the Near East, hand-building offered Cypriot potters a broader range of idiosyncratic expression, which fostered a variety of elaborate vessel forms, distinctive painted decoration, and a

Figure 16. Reconstructed pottery from Politiko-*Troullia*, including two large Red Polished Ware bowls (at back; note the mend hole drilled in the bowl on the left), smaller Red Polished and White Painted Ware bowls (in left and right foreground), and a White Painted Ware flask with an elaborate high loop handle.

certain whimsical flair expressed occasionally in stylized human or animal depictions (Figure 17).

Archaeologists working on Cyprus tend to categorize Bronze Age pottery according to ceramic "wares," each of which is defined by its clay, temper,[7] method of manufacture, and decoration (Stewart and Dikaios 1962). Over the course of our excavations, we recovered more than 175,000 potshards. Most of these shards represent fragments of Red Polished Ware vessels, which are characterized by their deep red, lustrously polished exterior surfaces (Frankel 1994). A second noteworthy, but much less abundant category consists of shards from White Painted Ware vessels, which are distinguished by clays that turned pale upon firing and elaborate light brown painted decoration. Both of these wares, accompanied by several others, were widespread across Cyprus during the Early and Middle Bronze ages. Red Polished vessels were particularly common in Bronze Age households on Cyprus, while the distinctive decoration of White Painted Ware made it an attractive commodity for trade across the Eastern Mediterranean (Charaf 2010).

---

7 "Temper" refers to particles of non-clay minerals (e.g., iron oxide or crushed potshards) or organic matter (e.g., straw or chaff) added to clay to prevent the shrinkage or cracking of a ceramic vessel during its drying and firing.

Figure 17. Leg of ceramic cooking tripod excavated from Politiko-*Troullia* West, decorated with possibly zoomorphic facial features.

Like all material evidence, archaeological ceramics can be analysed from many perspectives for a variety of purposes. Several factors make pottery particularly informative for archaeologists: potshards preserve well, are often abundant, and variations in pottery manufacture and style can indicate its place of manufacture, use, and time frame. Archaeologists analyse ceramics chronologically based on the principle that pottery vessels tend to change gradually according to people's shifting stylistic preferences through time. In the modern world, stylistic change is all around us, as exemplified by trends in the clothes we wear, the foods we eat, and the appearance of the cars we drive. Pottery was a common commodity in the ancient past that similarly would have changed stylistically through time. On this basis, archaeologists compare pottery styles between phases at one site or between multiple sites to build pottery chronologies that we use to infer which styles were earlier or later relative to one another. For example, Red Polished Ware was a hallmark pottery style through the Early and Middle Bronze Ages and constitutes most of the ceramics used at Politiko-*Troullia* (87% of shards from all six phases). White Polished Ware, on the other hand,

Figure 18. Basalt grinding stone excavated from Politiko-*Troullia* West, worn smooth from long-term use, for example by grinding cereal grains to prepare flour.

is a style more specific to the Middle Bronze Age. At Politiko-*Troullia*, it first appears as just three shards in Phase 3, then becomes increasingly abundant in later occupation phases at the site (reaching almost 8% of shards in Phases 1b and 1a).

3.1.2 Ground Stone Implements and Gameboards

Stone artifacts (largely basalt or limestone at Politiko-*Troullia*) were ground into a variety of forms that provide important insights on day-to-day activities. The hard surfaces of igneous stones were used for grinding grains (Figure 18). Large limestone cobbles were hollowed out to serve as mortars for processing olives and pounding raw materials such as copper ore. The Bronze Age of Cyprus also featured relatively large flat stones that were crafted into gameboards by pecking their surface to create shallow depressions for moveable pebbles or game pieces. Gameboards appear in two forms, both possibly introduced from Egypt (Swiny 1980, 1986). The more common board configuration uses a rectangular matrix of depressions (most often in a 3x10 pattern) known in Egyptian texts as *senet* ("passing;" Piccione 1990a) (Figure 19). A less standardized spiral pattern was known as *mehen* ("the coiled one," i.e., the game of the coiled serpent; Piccione 1990b) (Figure 20). Tokens may have been moved along these gameboards, perhaps by rolling cubically shaped sheep or goat

Figure 19. *Senet* gaming stone excavated from the Southern Courtyard of *Troullia* West with characteristic rectangular 10x3 pattern of shallow depressions pecked into a limestone slab.

knuckle bones (astragali), which were used as dice in antiquity (Perry-Gal et al. 2022). Interestingly, *senet* and *mehen* gaming stones were spread widely across our excavations, embedded in open courtyard spaces, in alley refuse, and reused in wall construction. Smaller, apparently more portable gaming stones were found in the terraced fields of Politiko-*Koliokremmos*. This relative ubiquity suggests that these gameboards were made, used, and discarded readily and repeatedly, and served as common focal points for socializing both in the settlement of *Troullia* and across the hillsides of *Koliokremmos*.

When I turn over my first gaming stone while excavating in Troullia West, I am struck by the care that someone took to peck the array of 30 depressions on the stone's surface so meticulously. I allow my imagination to take me back 4000 years and envision groups of friends huddled around a gameboard, rolling dice, moving their pieces, and sharing the latest news of their families, perhaps paralleling the neighbourly backgammon and card games played today in coffee houses across Cyprus.

3.1.3 Stone and Metal Tools

In the course of their everyday lives, the people of Politiko-*Troullia* would have needed cutting tools for a wide range of activities ranging from slaughtering animals to reaping and threshing crops, and carving wooden or bone artifacts. While the Bronze Age is celebrated (even by its very name) for the advent of metal technology, most of these tools were made of stone that was "knapped" to form sharp edges. Knapping creates cutting tools by striking a workable stone with a harder

Figure 20. *Mehen* gaming stone with spiral of shallow pecked depressions embedded in Southern Courtyard of Politiko-*Troullia* West, also shown in Figures 13 and 14.

hammerstone or pressuring it with a pointed tool made, for example, of deer antler. The majority of stone tools on Cyprus were knapped from chert, a form of crystalline quartz, which is found abundantly as nodules in the limestone bedrock across the island. This relatively simple technology allowed *Troullia*'s residents to readily produce an abundance of *ad hoc* cutting tools, which could be used for multiple tasks as long as they simply had a sharp edge. More formalized stone tools included long narrow blades with finely worked edges that were fitted ("hafted") into carved wooden or bone handles, for example to create sickles for harvesting crops. Repeated use would have led eventually to worn out or broken knives and sickles, which were discarded in abundance.

In contrast, the advent of metallurgy introduced much more demanding pyrotechnology to transform more strategic, less ubiquitous raw materials into formal tools for more specific tasks. Cyprus is renowned for its high-quality copper ore,[8] which would have been available in the geological formation of pillow lavas encircling the Troodos Mountain foothills (Kassianidou 2013), including deposits near Politiko-*Troullia*. However, the multi-stage metallurgical process of crushing ore, smelting molten copper at high temperature, and casting metal tools would have made copper metallurgy a dangerous resource-intensive technology with noxious and potentially toxic fumes and by-products. Further, the development of bronze metallurgy involved alloying copper, either with naturally co-occurring arsenic or imported tin. Arsenic would have introduced an additional, though possibly unrecognized health hazard, and tin is found in only a limited number of sources world-wide, none of which are on Cyprus. The nearest well-attested tin sources to Politiko-*Troullia* lay in southern Anatolia and Central Asia (e.g., Powell et al. 2024), so import of tin to Cyprus would have been logistically challenging and expensive. Thus, metal tools were the antithesis of chipped stone artifacts. Their production involved limited resources, great material cost, and a challenging technology. Unlike stone artifacts, worn out or broken metal tools could have been re-smelted for renewed use. However, copper and bronze tools and weapons, no matter how utilitarian, were highly prized and conserved, rather than readily discarded. As a result, metal artifacts tend to be underrepresented at archaeological sites,

8 In fact, the English word "copper" probably derives from the Latin *cuprum* and the term *aes cyprium*, or metal of Cyprus (Urbanus 2024).

which makes the graphic metallurgical evidence from Politiko-*Troullia* particularly striking!

3.1.4 Small Personal Possessions

A variety of intriguing details about personal life are illuminated by small artifacts recovered archaeologically after being lost or discarded inadvertently in the deep past. Remnants of jewellery include fragments of picrolite, a form of steatite prized for its workability and distinctive greenish hue. The only source for this mineral in Cyprus is on the upper slopes of Mt. Olympus, the island's highest peak, from which picrolite pebbles are washed and tumbled to the lower reaches of the Kouris and Karyotis riverbeds to the southwest (Xenophontos 1991). This limited source and its distance from most Bronze Age settlements, including Politiko-*Troullia*, made picrolite highly valued for personal ornamentation (Bolger 2003: 156). Archaeological recovery of picrolite artifacts from far flung sites across Cyprus suggests island-wide exchange of this precious commodity, especially as a means of signalling personal wealth in the Bronze Age. Other small, individualized artifacts attest to many less apparent craft activities. Awls, needles, and pins, with points and eyes finely crafted from animal bone or cast in copper, remind us of the importance of sewing and personal apparel, two aspects of day-to-day life that leave us tantalizingly minimal archaeological evidence.

Textile manufacture also has limited archaeological visibility but would have carried potentially major implications for trade relations and for signalling social identity. Chief indicators of this craft include spindle whorls and loom weights, both of which accompanied a major undercelebrated technological innovation: the introduction of the warp-weighted loom (Smith 2019). Spindle whorls are pierced weights that are positioned on a thin shaft, or spindle, which is rotated by hand to twist fibres into thread or yarn. Bronze Age spindle whorls are commonly ceramic and many Cypriot spindle whorls are distinguished by elaborate incised designs, which may have reflected stylistic preferences or, more intriguingly, signalled the social identities of the women and men who used them (Muti and Douglas 2019) (Figure 21). Warp-weighted looms use warp threads strung vertically to provide a tense, lengthwise structure for a woven article, while weft threads are woven horizontally through the warp. Bundles of warp threads are held taught by stone loom weights. Archaeologically, loom weights provide vestigial evidence of this technology, which otherwise leaves few tangible remains (Martensson et al. 2009).

Figure 21. Ceramic spindle whorls excavated from Politiko-*Troullia,* crafted from an assortment of differently coloured ceramic wares with a wide range of detailed incised decorative patterns.

Prior to joining this excavation, I had expected that artifacts would be rare discoveries. But after my first week of digging, trowelling, trimming, and sieving, I am starting to become overwhelmed by the amount of evidence we are excavating! Nevertheless, some of the artifacts I have found are particularly memorable. Amid a seemingly steady flow of potshards, I remember finding a large whitish fragment of a jar rim with unusually intricate brown painted designs. That afternoon, as we did at the end of

each dig day, we washed all our day's artifacts, and I brought this shard to the attention of our pottery analyst. Immediately animated, they rushed over to uncrate a jar that they had reconstructed from shards excavated last summer and showed me with breathless excitement that my shard completed the jar! They went on to explain that White Painted Ware vessels like this one were highly valued and widely traded across the Mediterranean in the Bronze Age! Wow, even a settlement as seemingly remote as Politiko-Troullia may have been trading far and wide, well beyond the shores of Cyprus!

A few days later I was sieving sediments we had excavated from the alleyway in Troullia West, when I glimpsed two tantalizing bits of distinctive green amid the pervasive brown background of my dig dirt. Carefully sorting through the pebbles and hardened earth, I picked out a broken thumb-sized fragment of picrolite and a complete copper sewing needle! Somehow, these artifacts struck a personal note with me, as I wondered if the picrolite had been part of someone's treasured, long-lost bracelet or necklace? And who used this needle, crafted of prized copper, rather than more common animal bone, to sew their family's garments or string a set of beads? It dawned on me that I was literally touching the lives of the anonymous but increasingly familiar inhabitants of Politiko-Troullia!

3.2 Ecofacts: Plant and Animal Evidence

Like an increasing number of archaeological projects today, our research at Politiko-*Troullia* has been ecologically oriented. For instance, based on our analysis of excavated ecofacts, we can reconstruct the Bronze Age landscape around Politiko-*Troullia* and how its occupants used it. Plant fragments preserve well if they are burned, in the form of charcoal from burned wood, or carbonized seeds from agricultural refuse. Archaeologists recover charcoal and seeds by using methods of flotation, in which we pour samples of excavated sediment (commonly multiple litres each) into a tank of water with a suspended mesh bottomed tub. Fine dirt settles to the tank's bottom, while charcoal and seeds float to the water's surface, where we recover them by skimming with a strainer. Heavier items like olive pits, small artifacts, or animal bone fragments are caught in the mesh bottomed tub. Archaeobotanists, who specialize in the analysis of archaeological plant remains, then view these remains under a microscope and identify the species and plant parts they represent. The plant species they identify indicate the crops cultivated by local farmers as well as carbonized parts of other plants that made up the natural vegetation around Politiko-*Troullia*. Similarly, zooarchaeologists analyse excavated animal bones to identify the species, skeletal part, age, and sex of the animals they represent (Figure 22). The resulting faunal data allow us to reconstruct how the villagers of Politiko-*Troullia* managed animals, including herding and penning of domesticated species, as well as hunting of wild animals in surrounding forests.

Figure 22. Identification, measurement, and analysis of animal bones excavated from Politiko-*Troullia* in our project lab in Pera Orinis.

As our excavation season stretches further towards summer, I look forward to any opportunity to cool off a bit. In the shade outside the lab, we wash all the buckets of artifacts we bring back from the field, which also removes a bit of the day's grit from our well-worn hands and arms. Whenever possible, I also like to help our archaeobotanist float our daily sediment samples (Figure 23). This necessitates much greater attention to detail, as we process each sample, carefully stirring through the muddy water, bringing burned plant remains to the surface, ranging from tiny charcoal fragments to individual wheat and barley grains, and whole olive pits. We finish each sample by picking through the heavy fragments that sink to the bottom of our mesh bottom tub, empty and clean the flotation tank, then refill it with clean water for the next sample. I am struck by how well preserved these burned remains are, and the details our archaeobotanists can identify! Likewise, some afternoons I help our zooarchaeologist sort dozens of bags of animal bones recovered through today's sieving. It is amazing how much information bones provide about the animals that the people of Politiko-Troullia once herded and hunted! My experiences helping in the lab make me realize how exacting these analyses are, and how they add an ecological dimension to our work stretching well beyond what I had expected before I joined this project!

Figure 23. Excavated archaeological sediment being poured into a metal flotation tank in the courtyard behind our project laboratory in the historic Pera Orinis girl's school building.

IV

The Story of Settlement at Politiko-*Troullia*

An overview of the phase-by-phase building and rebuilding of Politiko-*Troullia* highlights major aspects of life in this Bronze Age Cypriot community. The village's earliest excavated evidence comes from the lower-most layers in the alley of *Troullia* West, which date to the settlement's founding about 2050 BCE (at the beginning of Phase 5). This east-west passageway bounded the village on its south and offered villagers a gentle downslope path to Kamaras Creek. Here we can envision village men, women, and children carrying water jars to be filled or laundry to be washed in the creek waters, which ran at a level just below the foundations of village buildings, and much higher than the creek bottom today (Figure 24). The people of Politiko-*Troullia* would have depended on these waters for drinking, cooking, and cleaning from the very inception of their settlement through its ensuing generations. The alley also was important for the local population, and especially for archaeologists, as a convenient location for disposal of the rubbish created by community activities. Our excavation revealed layer upon layer of abundant personal refuse, ranging from intentionally discarded meal remains (for example, charcoal from fires, burned seeds from parching grain, and bones from dinners of roasted sheep and goat) to unintentionally lost personal items (for instance, bone and copper needles, and small perforated shells and stones from broken jewellry).

Figure 24. Portrait of architecture and activities in Politiko-*Troullia* West as inferred from excavated archaeological evidence, facing northeast. Activities included deer butchering, feasting, and socializing around a board game in the Southern Courtyard, and creek-side washing, spinning, and collection of water from Kamaras Creek. Community trash accumulated in the alleyway leading down to the creek. The intramural village well is shown at upper left (drawing by Gary James).

Between about 2020 and 2000 BCE (Phase 4), the community built a large complex that incorporated two courtyards on the north side of the alley, with creek-side rooms adjoining the courtyards on the west, and possibly additional rooms upslope on the east. These courtyards measured eight metres wide and 10 metres long, and we infer that they were unroofed open spaces for several reasons. At other excavated Bronze Age settlements, similarly large spaces are interpreted as unroofed, while roofed rooms rarely reach this size.[9] Likewise, an ethnoarchaeological

9 At Sotira *Kaminoudhia*, Marki *Alonia*, and Alambra *Mouttes*, roofed rooms are rarely wider than 4.5 metres (Coleman et al. 1996: fig.14; Swiny et al. 2003: figs. 2.16-2.18; Frankel and Webb 2006: figs. 11.1-11.8). On the other hand, large enclosures at Bronze Age sites measuring six or more metres wide are interpreted as unroofed exterior spaces (Swiny et al. 2003: 58; Frankel and Webb 2006: figs. 11.1-11.8).

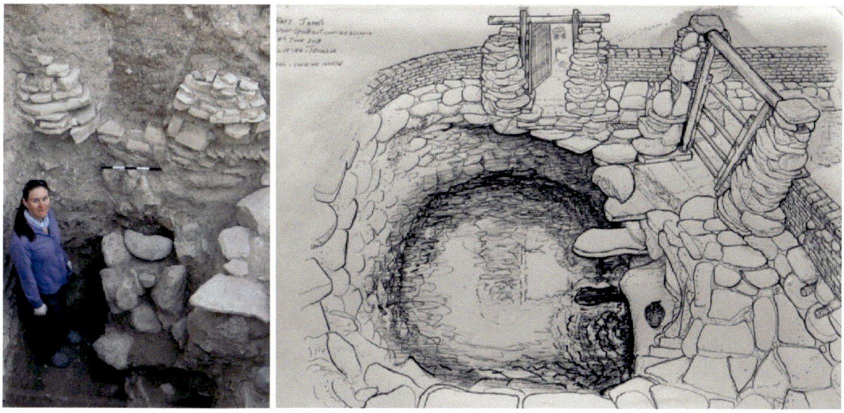

Figure 25. (Left) Photograph of excavated Bronze Age well in Politiko-*Troullia* West and (Right) artistic depiction of its original configuration (drawing by Gary James), both views facing north. Note the stone-pillared gateway shown in archaeological cross-section and reconstructed artistically. Two gates led to steps down to the water table, providing access to water for drinking, cooking, and washing.

study of traditional houses in one abandoned Cypriot village documented no roofed rooms larger than 3.5 metres wide (Swiny et al. 2003: 58).[10] Archaeologists often use parallels from historic and prehistoric studies like these to interpret their own evidence. On this basis, we can deduce that the courtyards at Politiko-*Troullia* were large open spaces, which, as we shall see, provided the settings for correspondingly important community-wide events!

Perhaps the most significant episode in Phase 4 featured the digging of a well in *Troullia* West. The well was accessed through gates on its north and east sides that opened to stone steps descending to the water table, which offered water filtered through natural sediments that may have made it safer for drinking than the stream flow of Kamaras Creek (Figure 25). The well remained in use through Phase 3, but Politiko-*Troullia*'s inhabitants significantly modified the architectural complex in *Troullia* West thereafter.

At about 1980 BCE (start of Phase 2), the architecture of *Troullia* West experienced a major disjunction when villagers relocated the walls of

10 Ethnoarchaeologists study the physical evidence of modern communities and the behaviour of their members to provide analogues for using archaeological evidence to infer prehistoric behaviour that we cannot observe.

Figure 26. (Top) Drone photograph showing incised Kamaras Creek along the western edge of Politiko-*Troullia* West, and (Bottom) artistic depiction of Bronze Age Politiko-*Troullia* and terraced hillside orchards on Politiko-*Koliokremmos* with Kamaras creek flowing at the base level of the village (drawing by Gary James), both views facing southeast.

the courtyards and their adjoining rooms about one metre upslope to the east. At this same time, the village well was abandoned and capped with hard-packed plaster, sealing off access to the former water source. This episode of reconstruction was triggered most likely by severe downcutting along Kamaras Creek, which carved a deep ravine, lowered

Figure 27. Artistic depiction of the compound in Politiko-*Troullia* East, facing west. Buildings of Politiko-*Troullia* West and North in background. Metallurgical activity in the courtyard at left foreground included smelting of copper ore at an open pit furnace, and casting of copper tools using tongs, crucibles, and carved stone moulds, including those excavated from Politiko-*Troullia* (drawing by Gary James).

its water level, and caused the well to dry up (Figure 26). This process also would have entailed pronounced erosion along the western edge of the settlement, forcing the relocation of buildings upslope to prevent stream erosion from undercutting their stone foundations. By relocating this part of their village upslope, the people of Politiko-*Troullia* may have been responding to significant environmental change on Cyprus just after 2000 BCE.

Following this reconstruction in Phase 2, life at Politiko-*Troullia* over the next few decades is attested by evidence from all three areas of excavation dating to Phases 1b, and 1a. A major highlight is a remarkable array of evidence for copper metallurgy from *Troullia* East between about 1960 and 1930 BCE (Phase 1b). In this compound, the front door of the main house opened to a passageway that led to a partially covered courtyard workspace (Figure 27). This courtyard

Figure 28. Carved limestone mould excavated from Politiko-*Troullia* East for casting copper daggers, chisels, and axe heads.

Figure 29. Copper alloy tongs excavated from Politiko-*Troullia* East for handling charcoal and crucibles during smelting of ore and casting of copper tools.

setting would have allowed airflow to ventilate the smoke and fumes that inevitably accompanied this potentially toxic pyrotechnic industry. In the courtyard, we recovered numerous chunks of unreduced copper ore in conjunction with a large pit furnace used to smelt the ore. We also discovered a carved limestone mould for casting three types of tools (Figure 28), fragments of the ceramic crucibles that were used to pour molten copper into this mould, a pair of copper alloy tongs (Figure 29) used to handle the crucibles and red-hot charcoal, as well as fragments of copper slag (a solidified by-product of smelting).

Likewise, in addition to the remains of a domed oven, *Troullia* North revealed the settlement's most abundant fragments of copper ore and slag, as well as fragments of terra cotta *tuyère*s (nozzles that were attached to a bellows to force air into a furnace). In sum, the collections of artifacts from *Troullia* East and North illustrate the full production sequence for smelting and casting an array of copper tools in two clearly defined metallurgical workshops at Politiko-*Troullia*.

The final episode at Politiko-*Troullia* in the years after about 1930 BCE (Phase 1a) is revealed by evidence of craft and communal activity adjacent to the courtyards of *Troullia* West (Figure 30). The interior of

Figure 30. Excavated remains of interior workspace in Politiko-*Troullia* West bounded by stone wall foundations and mudbrick-lined bins, with broken remains of large ceramic storage jars that were embedded in the floor, photo facing northeast.

Figure 31. Artistic depiction of compound excavated in Politiko-*Troullia* West shown in Figure 30. Mudbrick basins possibly used for dying textiles, and adjacent open area with a perforated stone base (possibly to anchor a ritual pole), decorated pottery vessels, and stone platform with painted fine ware juglets, all shown where excavated, facing southwest (drawing by Gary James).

this structure is marked by a series of rectangular mudbrick-lined basins set along the base of its walls (Figure 31). One intriguing possibility is that these basins may have been used for settling mineral-based liquid pigments derived from the numerous pieces of red and yellow ochre recovered in our excavations. We can take this interpretation one step further to suggest that pigments like these could have been used for dying textiles (Bombardieri and Muti 2018). To the north of this possible dye workshop lay open space with a large circular stone ring that could have provided the base for an upright pillar or pole. In the area around this base, we found a large rectangular altar-like stone slab and a burned earthen floor, both arrayed with the remains of finely crafted painted juglets. These remains mark the final event in the life story of Politiko-*Troullia* and carry intriguingly ritualistic connotations, since they feature offerings of highly visible prized pottery in a setting marked by ritual installations and a seemingly intentional conflagration. Perhaps most importantly, this evidence helps suggest that Politiko-*Troullia* and its role in Cypriot prehistory are not best appreciated simply in terms of a “village” in the traditional sense of a rural settlement that primarily provided agricultural sustenance for larger towns and cities. Instead, the full range of our evidence opens possibilities for reconstructing a community highly involved in a range of industrial and craft enterprises, some with clear potential for conveying social identity.

V

Plants, Animals, and Landscapes at Politiko-*Troullia*

We are now well into our field season, and I have a greater appreciation for the wide range of evidence we can use to envision the lives of the inhabitants of this Bronze Age community. During second breakfast today I gaze at the surrounding fields of planted barley and wild oats, at the olive groves of the nearby monastery, and at the sparsely wooded hills beyond them, and I wonder what the landscape around Politiko-Troullia looked like 4000 years ago, and how can we possibly figure out how people used it so long ago?

5.1 Botanical Remains, Crop Cultivation, and Local Vegetation

To reconstruct the cultivated crops and natural vegetation around Politiko-*Troullia*, we floated more than 50 samples of excavated sediment to recover more than 500 seeds and charcoal fragments (Klinge and Fall 2010; Falconer and Fall 2013; Fall et al. 2015). The most abundant seeds (about 80%) come from cultivated orchard plants, especially olive, but also including grape, fig, and wild pistachio. The remainder represent wild grasses and legumes (about 15%), while only a small proportion (about 5%) come from cultivated cereals like wheat, barley, oats, and rye.

How do burned seeds end up in archaeological deposits? Crushed olive pits provide a rich fuel source as a by-product of olive oil production (Rowan 2015). In fact, combustion of olive pits produces more energy than burning hardwood (Roots 2021). Seeds also may be burned unintentionally during crop processing and food preparation (Fuller and Harvey 2006; van der Veen 2007; Fuller and Stevens 2009). Although firewood appears to have been plentiful at Politiko-*Troullia*, seeds from many other plants eaten by livestock may be carbonized through the burning of animal dung (Klinge and Fall 2010; Shahack-Gross 2011), especially in other settlements with more limited wood resources. So, carbonized seeds provide direct evidence of the crops and orchards that were cultivated by the farmers of Politiko-*Troullia*, as well as the wild plants that accompanied these cultigens. All these forms of burning would have produced abundant refuse, so it is not surprising that more than 80% of our carbonized seeds were recovered from the trash-rich alley in *Troullia* West.

Archaeological charcoal, on the other hand, tells us more directly about the trees that provided firewood for Politiko-*Troullia* (Klinge and Fall 2010; Fall et al. 2015). A clear majority of the charcoal fragments we recovered and identified (64%) represent forest species, mostly pine, accompanied by lesser amounts of cypress, oak, and hawthorn. Charcoal from plane trees came from stream-side vegetation. Villagers also harvested and burned a substantial amount of wood pruned from their orchards, especially olive, plus small amounts of pomegranate. As with burned seeds, a sizeable proportion of our analysed charcoal was recovered from the alley. Wood burning was focused particularly in the courtyard of *Troullia East*, where we recovered more than 85% of our charcoal evidence as a distinct byproduct of local metallurgy.

We also expanded the scope of our analyses by combining our excavated botanical evidence, our local survey results, and scientific techniques in archaeology to reconstruct how the occupants of Politiko-*Troullia* made and utilized the landscape around their settlement. During our reconnaissance of the slopes of Politiko-*Koliokremmos* we mapped 102 stone terrace walls on hillsides that are carpeted with artifacts from the Bronze Age (Fall et al. 2012; Ridder et al. 2017). Today, longer terrace walls still retain soil in small arable plots, while shorter walls directly overlooking the settlement were constructed to hold back hill slope erosion. We categorized these walls into six types based on their construction and their incorporation of artifacts. Among these wall types, four represent historically recent construction, but two types of heavily lichen-covered stone walls offer a glimpse of ancient agricultural terrace construction. One type was chinked with fragments of terra cotta tiles, which may have covered the roof of a long-lost Medieval building that once crowned the summit of Politiko-*Koliokremmos*. The other type incorporates Red Polished Ware potshards as chinking or in their foundation sediments. We hypothesize that these two types of terrace walls were built by local farmers in antiquity who cultivated the fields they cradled on the slopes overlooking Politiko-*Troullia*. Other accounts of ancient Cypriot field systems (Deckers 2003; Noller and Wells 2003) describe terrace walls that appear to date as early as the Hellenistic Period (325-58 BCE; Held 2003). However, many of the walls and fields on Politiko-*Koliokremmos* may date even earlier to the Bronze Age and potentially could represent some of the earliest evidence of terraced agriculture, especially for cultivating olives and grapes, on the island of Cyprus!

5.2 Animal Bones, Herding, and Hunting

The animal bones discarded by the villagers of Politiko-*Troullia* provide a direct indication of their herding and hunting practices, as well as another avenue for reconstructing the local landscape (Falconer and Fall 2013; Metzger et al. 2021). Analysis of more than 8500 excavated bones indicates herding of domesticated sheep and goats, two mainstays of Mediterranean animal management in the past and present, which are represented by more than 60% of the identified bones from Politiko-*Troullia*. These herds would have provided meat, as well as wool (from sheep) and dairy products (from goats) for local consumption as well as for marketable products like textiles. Other, less numerous domesticates included cattle and equids (probably donkeys) that potentially would have offered both meat and traction for pulling ploughs. The people of Politiko-*Troullia* also were active hunters, judging from the substantial frequencies of bones from wild Mesopotamian fallow deer (almost 24%) and feral pigs (almost 5%). Small numbers of fox bones and one bone from a barn owl indicate other wild animals on the landscape, while a few canine bones show that dogs hovered around the settlement and perhaps provided some household companionship.

We have also applied the exciting method of stable isotope analysis[11] to explore how local villagers managed the cultivated and natural

11 Isotopes are alternative forms of the same element that differ in the number of neutrons in their nuclei. They may be radioactive or stable (non-radioactive). They are identified numerically according to their differing atomic masses.

landscapes around their community (Pilaar Birch et al. 2022).[12] Our results indicate that cattle, goats, and sheep ate substantial amounts of cultivated crops, in addition to grazing on grasses. Cattle and sheep were managed intensively, possibly including grazing on manured fields or feeding of penned animals. Goats, however, browsed more freely on both cultivated crops and wild vegetation. In stark contrast, deer and pig consumed a diet of wild plants, with little consumption of cultivated crops. These results allow us to reconstruct a community engaged in sheep, goat and cattle husbandry on limited local fields, and nearby intensive management of terraced hillside orchards, beyond which stretched pine/oak forested foothills populated with huntable deer and swine.

In concert, the data from agricultural terraces, plant remains, and animal bones allow us to envision a multi-faceted landscape moulded by the settlers of Politiko-*Troullia*, which provided the resources that attracted them to this locality for multiple centuries (Figure 32). Fields of annual crops, represented primarily by wheat and barley, may have been manured, and probably lay within and around the settlement. Their locations and ownership may have shifted latterly through time, in keeping with the tendency for the structures in Cypriot Bronze Age settlements to be built, rebuilt and abandoned. Amid and around the settlement, shepherds would have managed the grazing of sheep and cattle closely, both in fields and pens. The immediately adjacent hillsides of Politiko-*Koliokremmos* were covered with pockets of intensively managed terraced orchards (primarily olive) that provided products that have long been integral to the Mediterranean diet that is so deeply rooted among the people of Cyprus, past and present. Goats were allowed to range more freely across fields and orchards, and perhaps on the hill slopes stretching past the settlement. Beyond the fields and orchards around Politiko-*Troullia* lay woodlands of pine and oak offering the fuelwood necessary for household cooking and heating fires, and for the industrial pyrotechnology practiced by village inhabitants. These forest lands likewise offered further food sources through the hunting of wild animals, featuring boar especially along upland creeks and streams, and herds of fallow deer extending into the increasingly high elevation slopes of the Troodos Mountains.

---

12 Our analyses of 21 wheat and barley seeds, and of 130 bones from both domesticated and wild animals measured the relative amounts of the stable carbon isotopes ^{13}C and ^{12}C, expressed as the ratio $\delta^{13}C$, which can indicate differences in the availability of water for crops. We also measured the ratio of the nitrogen isotopes ^{15}N and ^{14}N, expressed as $\delta^{15}N$, which can show variation in ancient crop management (especially fertilization).

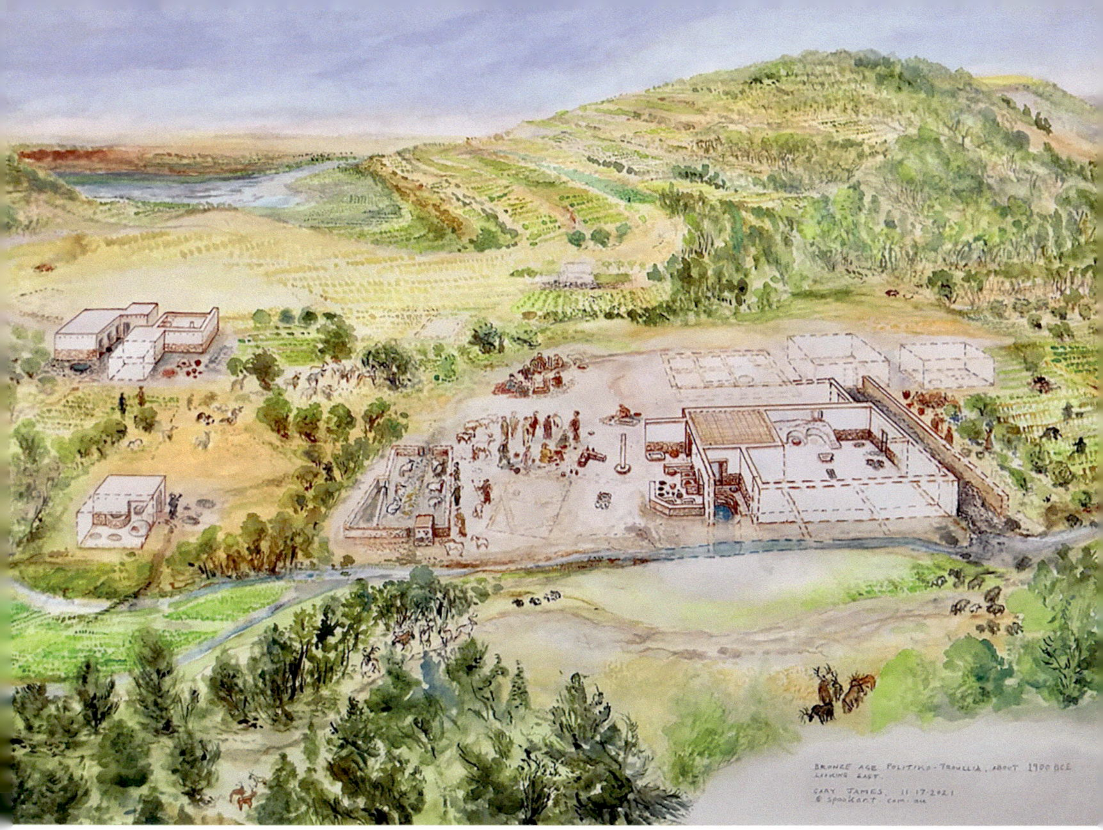

Figure 32. Artistic portrait of the Bronze Age settlement of Politiko-*Troullia* at the foot of the terraced hill slopes of Politiko-*Koliokremmos*, facing east. In the foreground Kamaras Creek flows along the western edge of the settlement, while the Pediaios River lies in the distance to the east. *Troullia* West in right foreground, *Troullia* North in left foreground, *Troullia* East in left background. The village, its fields, pastures, and terraced orchards, lie on the verge of pine-oak woodlands with feral pigs and wild Mesopotamian fallow deer (artwork by Gary James).

We have reached the final week of this year's fieldwork. At the end of my day of excavation, I hike roughly two kilometres from the site down the dry Pediaios riverbed to the historic girl's school building in Pera where our project cook has delivered today's lunch and dinner. Along with my fellow project members, we enjoy multiple helpings of her Cypriot cooking at long tables on the schoolhouse front porch. We particularly appreciate her hearty lunchtime soups, which rehydrate us after working seven hours in the sun, during lunches animated by enthusiastic conversations about today's newest discoveries. After lunch, I check the chore list to see that I am scheduled to wash the lunch dishes. Along with a fellow project member, we tackle our assignment right away so that we can find more adventurous afternoon activities! I volunteer to help our project geographer pilot a remotely controlled drone, or unmanned aerial vehicle (UAV), to take detailed aerial photographs covering the Troullia/Koliokremmos landscape. They fly our small project drone, which has four rotors and carries a miniature camera, during the late afternoon, when breezes subside and soft lighting works well for photography. Skilfully hovering the UAV 30 metres above the ground, buzzing like an angry oversized bee, they take thousands of high-resolution overhead photos. Our geographic modeller subsequently "stitched" more than 1300 of these images together electronically to create a high-resolution composite image (Ridder et al. 2023), which enables us to envision and analyse the physical landscape on which the people of Politiko-Troullia carried out their daily lives.

VI

Politiko-*Troullia*: A Portrait of Life in the Bronze Age

6.1 Social Identity in Bronze Age Cyprus

Based on all our discoveries, I can start to put myself in the shoes of a Troullia villager and imagine how they lived their lives here on a day-to-day basis. Picturing myself in this setting 4000 years ago, I wonder further what kinds of special occasions these early Cypriots celebrated together?

The identification of social groups in the deep past is an enduring challenge for ancient historians, let alone for scholars investigating prehistoric communities such as those of Bronze Age Cyprus. However, while we may not be able to definitively identify the ethnic groups who lived on prehistoric Cyprus or how they referred to themselves, we can discern considerable evidence of how they celebrated their communal social identity at Politiko-*Troullia*. The remains discovered in the Southern Courtyard of *Troullia* West provide dramatic evidence for an array of activities potentially involving many community members of Politiko-*Troullia*. As we noted previously, the alley was used to discard the full spectrum of village rubbish, particularly smaller artifacts, numerous seeds, and abundant bones from the entire range of domesticated and wild animals. Turning from the alley into the Southern Courtyard, we are confronted with a striking assemblage of animal bones and artifacts, which jointly suggest how Cypriot communities may have signalled and celebrated their social identity four millennia ago.

Figure 33. Red Polished Ware pitcher (known as an *askos*) in the form of a quail, used for pouring ritual libations. Excavated from the Southern Courtyard in *Troullia* West; its missing spout would have been rendered as the quail's head.

Singularly special artifacts include a nearly complete *askos* (a zoomorphic ritual pitcher for pouring oil) in the form of a bird, most likely a quail or partridge (Figure 33). Most strikingly, this courtyard revealed the highest density of animal bones anywhere at Politiko-*Troullia*, including the most abundant remains of wild animals. This evidence fits well with the characteristics of communal feasting deduced by other archaeologists (Dietler 2001; Steel 2002, 2004), including highly concentrated deposition of bones, a pronounced focus on a primary food source, and skeletal parts indicating conspicuous consumption. The bones from the Southern Courtyard include entire animal skeletons, especially of Mesopotamian fallow deer. The discard of deer foot bones, for example, suggests that the full process of skinning and butchering entire carcasses was carried out repeatedly in the Southern Courtyard. This portrait of deer consumption suggests that Cypriots hunted Mesopotamian fallow deer "in a controlled, sustainable way within a system of management," culling young males from deer populations in the same manner as from domestic sheep herds (Croft 2002: 175). This strategy not only maximized the exploitation of animal resources, but it also allowed for clear expression of social identity. Feasting continues to play an important role in modern society if you stop to consider how we celebrate special occasions by gathering in family or community groups to share a particularly large meal, often featuring special foods and drinks, which may be specified according to the occasion being celebrated. Politko-*Troullia* provides distinct archaeological evidence of exactly this type of feasting behaviour four millennia ago, as ancient Cypriot society gradually coalesced to form a shared social foundation for civilization on their island.

The evidence for social expression from the Southern Courtyard is compounded by several forms of artifacts, including pronounced deposition of spindle whorls and distinct patterning of large groundstone implements (Falconer and Fall 2013; Falconer et al. 2014). A large, embedded gaming stone represents an intentionally situated location for group socializing, while spinning and weaving offered highly visible media for conveying social identity. On Cyprus, the very act of spinning provided an opportunity to show who you are, as symbolized by the island's characteristic decorated spindle whorls, and no doubt by the sewn and woven goods worn by Politiko-*Troullia*'s inhabitants.

Perhaps the most evocative form of evidence from the Southern Courtyard features abundant fragments of thin ceramic plank figures, which portray individual humans with highly depictive facial features (Figure 34). These figures provide poignant indications of how Bronze Age Cypriots may have signalled their identities as individuals or as members of a social group within their larger communities (a Campo 1994; Knox 2012). These portraits feature thin, rectangular, two-dimensional depictions of the human form made from the same ceramic wares used for Cypriot pottery. The Politiko-*Troullia* plank figures conform to a standard anthropomorphic style found on Cyprus, with a neckless rectangular head on a larger rectangular body and minimal or no appendages (see Falconer and Fall 2013: fig. 11; a Campo 1994). They would have ranged in height between about 15 and 20 centimetres. The most expressive *Troullia* examples have distinct individualized facial features and incised decoration that represents hair, jewellery, clothing, tattoos, or body paint. In other words, through their individualized features these figures truly bring their Bronze Age subjects to life!

While ceramic plank figures have been found at archaeological sites across Cyprus, the Southern Courtyard of Politiko-*Troullia* offers the only example of a large stone plank figure excavated on Cyprus (Figure 35). This unique human depiction stands in contrast to ceramic plank figurines by virtue of its greater height (38 centimetres) and its carved limestone manufacture. This limestone slab has been shaped with two slightly asymmetrical appendages representing arms or shoulders. Longitudinal striations show that the front of the figure has been scraped flat, with a cluster of horizontal incised lines about 10 centimetres from the bottom

Figure 34. Head of an anthropomorphic ceramic plank figure excavated from the Southern Courtyard in Politiko-*Troullia* West, with finely detailed portraiture of an individual's eyes, nose, eye lashes, eyebrows, and hair.

of the figure, and punctate marks near the top that may indicate eyes. Only 13 stone plank figures have been reported previously from Cyprus, and this example from Politiko-*Troullia* is the only fully documented stone plank figure excavated from a Bronze Age settlement on the island (Falconer et al. 2014).

Most previously excavated Cypriot plank figures have been recovered from Bronze Age tombs, leading to their interpretation as religious idols or substitute entombment figures associated with elite members of society (Talalay and Cullen 2002; Bolger 2003; Keswani 2005). In contrast, the ceramic and stone figures from the settlement of Politiko-*Troullia* open an alternative interpretation suggesting that plank figures provided evocative expressions of group identity. These figures may have been positioned prominently upright with their unadorned lower portions dug into an earthen surface (Knox 2012). As a case in point, the stone plank figure from Politiko-*Troullia* was found lying face down near the entrance to the Southern Courtyard in Phase 4, as if its emplacement there would have guarded the entrance to this important communal space.

Plank figures also convey intriguing behavioural implications based on their sexual ambiguity, and potential ornamentation. Although some have modest breasts, the gender of most ceramic plank figures remains unclear (Talalay and Cullen 2002; Knox 2012). Stone plank figures also may represent varied identities over the course of their use lives. For example, painted decoration could have been applied, removed, or

5 cm

Figure 35. Limestone plank figure excavated just inside the Phase 4 entrance to the Southern Courtyard in Politiko-*Troullia* West. Note its shaved surface and very stylized human form with rectangular head, abbreviated appendages, and horizontal striations just below the figure's waist.

renewed according to varying occasions. Likewise, the near absence of carved details on the *Troullia* stone figure suggests that its identity might have been signalled with clothing or jewellery, as is also suggested by the incised decoration of ceramic plank figures. The depictive ambiguity of stone plank figures could allow a single figure to convey multiple social identities, representing different individuals or different phases or events in an individual's life (Hendrix 2003). Based on their symbolic richness and material uniformity, plank figures reveal tantalizing hints of social group identities. In sum, the Southern Courtyard at Politiko-*Troullia* provided open space for many communal activities, including food processing (large ground-stone platforms), leisurely diversions (carved gaming stones), textile manufacture (spindle whorls and loom weights), and social recognition (plank figures). All of these activities were incorporated with conspicuous feasting on Mesopotamian fallow deer by the people of Politiko-*Troullia*, as a potentially powerful means of signalling their social identity.

6.2 Exploring the Pre-Urban Foundations for Cypriot Civilization

Our study of Politiko-*Troullia* vividly illustrates life in a multi-faceted community and its surrounding landscape about 4000 years ago. In keeping with best scientific tradition, we have integrated multiple lines of investigation to portray ways of life significantly different from our own based on highly fragmentary data. We hope that the resulting portrait brings a new-found remembrance of the daily lives and celebratory occasions experienced here in the deep past, and the legacy of these lives for the people of modern Cyprus. One important and sometimes overlooked virtue of science is its capacity to produce unexpected results, in this case to illuminate a community that was not a village in the conventional agrarian sense of the term. Instead, the importance of Politiko-*Troullia* lay not in its size or its agricultural production, but in a variety of industries and activities that figured prominently as organizing principles in pre-urban Cyprus: copper metallurgy, textile production, and the development of social cohesion and identity that is signalled clearly by communal feasting. In sum, this community illustrates the facets of ancient Cyprus that make the island's preurban legacy distinctly different from those of neighbouring regions. This legacy distinguishes the deep past of Cyprus and makes it of enduring significance for understanding the preurban roots of Cypriot civilization.

After the first few days of fieldwork, I looked forward to returning to the comforts of modern civilization, especially hot showers and clean clothes. But now the end of our field season is approaching all too rapidly, and I realize how I will miss the hard work, the camaraderie, and the inspiration of each day's new insights on life in Cyprus in the deep past of the Bronze Age. Like most of my fellow excavators, I came to this project with only modest knowledge of how we can reconstruct past lives, communities, and landscapes. However, I am leaving with newfound inspiration for scientific exploration, and its potential to open new insights on the world around us, past, present, and future. Little did I realize how I would come to treasure what we have found here at Politiko-Troullia, how we can interpret our findings to shed light on the lives of our forebears in the distant past, and the ways those lives provided the foundation for Cypriot civilization. I am already plotting a return to Cyprus, and who knows...? I may soon forget the challenges of life in the field and return for another season or even consider building a career investigating the mysteries of the distant past! Not only am I hooked, but I also hope our work at Politiko-Troullia will similarly inspire a new generation of prehistoric scientists to study the wonders of ancient Cyprus!

Acknowledgements

The research described here was made possible by the enthusiastic hard work contributed in the field and lab by nearly 200 project members, including undergraduates, post-graduates, and staff, who joined us from Cyprus, the US, Australia, Canada and Poland. Principal Analysts included Mary Metzger (zooarchaeology), Mara Horowitz and Eilis Monahan (ceramics), Elizabeth Ridder (geographic information scientist and drone pilot), Chris Galletti (geographic modelling), Suzanne Pilaar Birch (stable isotope analysis), Steven Porson and Joanna Klinge (archaeobotany), John Hunt (soil resistivity), Gary James (artwork), Helen Juergens (data management and lab photography), Rachel Benkowski (photography), John Czarzasty (fieldwork manager), Sid Rempel (field photography), Frank Garrod (field equipment and logistics), and Monika Monici (cook). Our work at Politiko-*Troullia* and *Koliokremmos* was conducted under permit from the Department of Antiquities of the Republic of Cyprus. We thank former Directors Dr. Pavlos Flourentzos, Dr. Maria Hadjicosti, Dr. Marina Solomidou-Ieronymidou, Dr. Despina Pilides, and current Director Dr. Giorgos Georgiou for their support and encouragement. Project funding was provided by research grants from the U.S. National Science Foundation (grants 0613760, 1031527, 1850259, 2114406, 2336739), the National Geographic Society, the American Society of Overseas Research, the University of North Carolina Charlotte, La Trobe University, and Arizona State University. The Cyprus American Archaeological Research Institute (CAARI), its former Directors Dr. Thomas Davis and Dr. Andrew McCarthy, its current Director Dr. Lindy Crewe, the CAARI staff, and our friends and colleagues in our host community of Pera Orinis (especially Ioannis Demetriades, Vasilis Vasiloudes, Tonia Bayada, Phil and Maria Menikefs, and former mayors Michaelis Tringides, Costas Miliotis, and Soulla Maoy Partasi) provided collegial hospitality. This book was written with the support of a Fulbright US Scholar grant (to SF) while the authors stayed at Elaia, the home of Thecla and Simon Perkins in Lythrodontas, Cyprus. Finally, this project and our careers would not have been possible without the unwavering encouragement of our parents, Judy and Bob Falconer, Barbara and Sam Fall, and the cheerful and willing participation of our sons Will and Sam Falconer.

References

a Campo AL. 1994. Anthropomorphic Representations in Prehistoric Cyprus: A Formal and Symbolic Analysis of Figurines, c. 3500-1800 B.C. Studies in Mediterranean Archaeology, Pocket-book 109. Jonsered: Paul Åströms Förlag.

Andreou GM. 2019. Socioeconomics of agrarian production: considering rural cooperatives in the archaeology of the eastern Mediterranean through the lens of 2nd millennium BCE Cyprus. World Archaeology 51: 291-310.

Artzy M, Perlman I, Asaro F. 1976. Alašiya of the Amarna Letters. Journal of Near Eastern Studies 35: 171-182.

Baldi J, Roux V. 2016. The innovation of the potter's wheel: a comparative perspective between Mesopotamia and the southern Levant. Levant 48(3): 236-253.

Bevan A, Conolly J. 2011. Terraced fields and Mediterranean landscape structure: an analytical case study from Antikythera, Greece. Ecological Modelling 222: 1303-1314.

Bolger DL. 2003. Gender in Ancient Cyprus. Narratives of Social Change on a Mediterranean Island. Walnut Creek, CA: Altamira Press.

Bombardieri L, Muti G. 2018. Erimi *Laonin Tou Porakou*. A textile community of practice in Middle Bronze Age Cyprus. Fasciculi Archaeologiae Historicae 31: 25-38.

Charaf H. 2010. Cypriot imported pottery from the Middle Bronze Age in Lebanon. Berytus 53-54: 147-165.

Coleman JE, Barlow JA, Mogelonsky MK, Schaar KW. 1996. Alambra: A Middle Bronze Age Settlement in Cyprus. Archaeological Investigations by Cornell University 1974-1985. Studies in Mediterranean Archaeology 118. Jonsered: Paul Åströms Förlag.

Crewe L. 2017. Interpreting settlement function and scale during MC III – LC IA using old excavations and new: Western Cyprus and Kisonerga (Kissonerga) Skalia in context. In: Pilides D, Mina M, editors. Four Decades of Hiatus in Archaeological Research in Cyprus: Towards Restoring the Balance. Studies on Ancient Cyprus 2, pp. 140-152. Vienna: Verlag Holzhausen.

Croft PW. 2002. Game management in early prehistoric Cyprus. Zeitschrift für Jagdwissenschaft 48: 172-179.

Deckers K. 2003. The Western Cyprus Geoarchaeological Survey: some case studies. In: Brysbaert A, de Bruijn N, Gibson E, Michael A, Monaghan M, editors. Symposium on Mediterranean Archaeology 2002, pp. 27-34. British Archaeological Reports, International Series 1142. Oxford: Archaeopress.

Dietler M. 2001. Theorizing the feast: rituals of consumption, commensal politics, and power in African contexts. In: Dietler M, Hayden B, editors. Feasts: Archaeological and Ethnographic Perspectives on Food, Politics, and Power, pp. 65-114. Washington, DC: Smithsonian Institution Press.

Dumper M, Stanley BE, Abu-Lughod JL. 2006. Cities of the Middle East and North Africa. London: Bloomsbury.

Falconer SE, Fall PL. 2013. Household and community behavior at Bronze Age Politiko-*Troullia*, Cyprus. Journal of Field Archaeology 38(2): 101-119. DOI:10.1179/0093469013Z.00000000041.

Falconer SE, Fall PL, Davis TW, Horowitz MT, Hunt J. 2005. Initial archaeological investigations at Politiko-*Troullia*. Report of the Department of Antiquities, Cyprus 2005: 69-85.

Falconer SE, Fall PL, Hunt J, Metzger, MC. 2012. Agrarian Settlement at Politiko-*Troullia*, 2008. Report of the Department of Antiquities, Cyprus 2010: 183-198.

Falconer SE, Monahan EM, Fall PL. 2014. A stone plank figure from Politiko-*Troullia*, Cyprus: potential implications for inferring Bronze Age communal behavior. Bulletin of the Schools of Oriental Research 371: 3-16.

Falconer SE, Ridder E, Pilaar Birch SE, Fall PL. 2023. Prehistoric Bronze Age radiocarbon chronology at Politiko-*Troullia*, Cyprus. Radiocarbon 65: 97-119. DOI:10.1017/RDC.2022.99.

Fall PL, Falconer SE, Galletti C, Schirmang T, Ridder E, Klinge JM. 2012. Long-term agrarian landscapes in the Troodos foothills, Cyprus. Journal of Archaeological Science 39: 2335-2347. DOI:10.1016/j.jas.2012.02.010.
Fall PL, Falconer SE, Horowitz MT, Hunt J, Metzger MC, Ryter D. 2008. Bronze Age settlement and landscape of Politiko-*Troullia*, 2005-2007. Report of the Department of Antiquities, Cyprus 2008: 183-208.
Fall PL, Falconer SE, Klinge JM. 2015. Bronze Age fuel use and its implications for agrarian landscapes in the eastern Mediterranean. Journal of Archaeological Science Reports 4: 182-191. DOI:10.1016/j.jasrep.2015.09.004.
Frankel D. 1994. Color variation on Cypriot Red Polished pottery. Journal of Field Archaeology 21(2): 205-219.
Frankel D, Webb JM. 2006. Marki Alonia. An Early and Middle Bronze Age Settlement in Cyprus. Excavations 1995-2000. Studies in Mediterranean Archaeology 123.2. Sävedalen: Paul Åstroms Förlag.
Fuller DQ, Harvey EL. 2006. The archaeobotany of Indian pulses: identification, processing and evidence for cultivation. Environmental Archaeology 11(2): 219-246.
Fuller DQ, Stevens CJ. 2009. Agriculture and the development of complex societies: an archaeobotanical agenda. In: Fairbairn AS, Weiss E, editors. From Foragers to Farmers. pp. 37-57. Oxford: Oxbow Books.
Galletti CS, Ridder E, Falconer SE, Fall PL. 2013. Maxent modeling of ancient and modern agricultural terraces in the Troodos foothills, Cyprus. Applied Geography 39: 46-56. DOI:10.1016/j.apgeog.2012.11.020.
Gates C. 2003. Ancient Cities: The Archaeology of Urban Life in the Ancient Near East and Egypt, Greece and Rome. London: Routledge.
Given M, Knapp AB. 2003. The Sydney Cyprus Survey Project: Social Approaches to Regional Archaeological Survey. Monumenta Archaeologica 21. Los Angeles: Cotsen Institute of Archaeology, University of California Los Angeles.
Goren Y, Bunimovitz S, Finkelstein I, Na'aman N. 1993. The location of Alashiya, petrographic analysis of the tablets. American Journal of Archaeology 107: 233-255.
Held SO. 2003. The regional archaeological survey. In: Swiny S, editor. Sotira Kaminoudhia: An Early Bronze Age Site in Cyprus. pp. 467-474. CAARI Monograph Series 4. ASOR Archaeological Reports 8. Boston: American Schools of Oriental Research.
Hendrix E. 2003. Painted Early Cycladic figures: an exploration of context and meaning. Hesperia 72: 405-46.

Kassianidou V. 2013. The exploitation of the landscape: metal resources and the copper trade during the age of the Cypriot city-kingdoms. Bulletin of the American Schools of Oriental Research 370: 49-82.
Keswani PS. 2005. Death, prestige, and copper in Bronze Age Cyprus. American Journal of Archaeology 109: 341-401.
Klinge JM, Fall PL. 2010. A paleoethnobotanical analysis of Bronze Age land use and land cover in the eastern Mediterranean. Journal of Archaeological Science 37: 2622-2629. DOI:10.1016/j.jas.2010.05.022.
Knapp AB. 2013. The Archaeology of Cyprus: From Earliest Prehistory Through the Bronze Age. Cambridge: Cambridge University Press.
Knox D-K. 2012. Making Sense of Figurines in Bronze Age Cyprus: A Comprehensive Analysis of Cypriot Ceramic Figurative Material from EC I – LC IIIA (c. 2300 BC – c.1100 BC). PhD thesis, Faculty of Humanities, University of Manchester.
Krahtopoulou A, Frederick C. 2008. The stratigraphic implications of long-term terrace agriculture in dynamic landscapes: polycyclic terraces from Kythera Island, Greece. Geoarchaeology 23: 550-585.
Manning SW. 2013. Cyprus at 2200 BC: rethinking the chronology of the Cypriot Early Bronze Age. In: Knapp AB, Webb JM, McCarthy A, editors. J.R.B. Stewart. An Archaeological Legacy. pp. 1-21. Studies in Mediterranean Archaeology CXXXIX. Uppsala: Åstroms Förlag.
Manning SW. 2019. Environment and sociopolitical complexity on prehistoric Cyprus: observations, trajectories, and sketch. In: Kearns C, Manning SW, editors. New Directions in Cypriot Archaeology. pp. 99-130. Ithaca, NY: Cornell University Press.
Mansel P. 2016. Aleppo: The Rise and Fall of Syria's Great Merchant City. London: Bloomsbury.
Martensson L, Nosch M-L, Strand EA. 2009. Shape of things: understanding a loom weight. Oxford Journal of Archaeology 28(4): 373-398.
Metzger MC, Ridder E, Pilaar Birch SE, Falconer SE, Fall PL. 2021. Animal exploitation and community behavior at a Middle Bronze village on Cyprus. In: Daujat J, Hadjikoumis A, Berthon R, Chahoud J, Kassianidou V, Vigne J-D, editors. Archaeozoology of Southwest Asia and Adjacent Areas XIII: Proceedings of the Thirteenth International Symposium, University of Cyprus, Nicosia, Cyprus, June 7-10, 2017. Volume 3, pp. 113-128. Atlanta, GA: Lockwood Press. DOI:10.2307/j.ctv2d7x51d.11.
Muti G, Douglas S. 2019. A case of identity. Investigating the symbolism of spindle whorls in Early and Middle Cypriot tombs. In: Żebrowska K, Ulanowska A, Lewartowski K, editors. Sympozjum Egejskie,

volume 2. pp. 19-30. Papers in Aegean Archaeology. Warsaw: Institute of Archaeology, University of Warsaw.
Noller J, Wells L. 2003. Mitsero Lambadhiotissa: check dams and Byzantine Church. In: Given M, Knapp AB, editors. The Sydney Cyprus Survey Project. Social Approaches to Regional Archaeological Survey. pp. 187-192. Monumenta Archaeologica 21. Los Angeles: Cotsen Institute of Archaeology, University of California Los Angeles.
Peltenburg E. 1993. Settlement discontinuity and resistance to complexity in Cyprus, ca. 4500-2500 B.C.E. Bulletin of the American Schools of Oriental Research 292: 9-23.
Perry-Gal L, Stern I, Erlich A. 2022. Gaming and divination in the Hellenistic Levant: the case study of the astragalus assemblage from Maresha, Israel. Levant 54(1): 65-79.
Piccione PA. 1990a. The Historical Development of the Game of Senet and its Significance for Egyptian Religion. PhD dissertation, Department of Near Eastern Languages and Civilizations, University of Chicago.
Piccione PA. 1990b. Mehen, mysteries, and resurrection from the coiled serpent. Journal of the American Research Center in Egypt 27: 43-52.
Pilaar Birch SE, Metzger MC, Ridder E, Porson S, Falconer SE, Fall PL. 2022. Herd management and subsistence practices as inferred from isotopic analysis of animals and plants at Bronze Age Politiko-*Troullia*, Cyprus. PLoS One, October 26, 2022. DOI:10.1371/journal.pone.0275757.
Powell W, Yener KA, Barjamovic G, Kulakoğlu F, Yazgan E, Mathur R. 2024. Tin isotopes reveal changing patterns of tin trade, connectivity and consumption from Anatolia and Central Asia at Kültepe. Journal of Archaeological Science 162: 105917.
Reimer PJ. 2022. The evolution of radiocarbon calibration. Radiocarbon 64(3): 523-539.
Ridder E, Galletti CS, Fall PL, Falconer SE. 2017. Economic and social activities on ancient Cypriot terraced landscapes. Journal of Environmental Management 202(3): 514-523. DOI:10.1016/j.jenvman.2016.12.037.
Ridder E, Fall PL, Falconer SE. 2023. Photogrammetric and GIS-based modeling of rapid sediment erosion and deposition on the taskscape of Bronze Age Politiko-*Troullia*, Cyprus. In: Ben-Yosef E, Jones IWN, editors. "And in Length of Days Understanding" (Job 12:12): Essays on Archaeology in the Eastern Mediterranean and Beyond in Honor of Thomas E. Levy. pp.1603-1624. Interdisciplinary Contributions to Archaeology. Cham: Springer. DOI:10.1007/978-3-031-27330-8_68.

Roots S. 2021. Spanish study reveals olive pit biofuel potential. Olive Oil Times. December 9, 2021.
Rowan E. 2015. Olive oil pressing waste as a fuel source in antiquity. American Journal of Archaeology 119(4): 465-482.
Shahack-Gross R. 2011. Herbivorous livestock dung: formation, taphonomy, methods for identification, and archaeological significance. Journal of Archaeological Science 38: 205-218.
Smith JS. 2019. Changes in weaving on the warp-weighted loom on Cyprus. Cahier du Centre d'Études Chypriotes 49: 129-144.
Steel L. 2002. Wine, women and song: drinking ritual in Cyprus in the Late Bronze and Early Iron Ages. In: Bolger D, Serwint, N, editors. Engendering Aphrodite: Women and Society in Ancient Cyprus. pp. 105-119. American Schools of Oriental Research Archaeological Reports 7; Cyprus American Archaeological Research Institute Monograph Series 3. Boston: American Schools of Oriental Research.
Steel L. 2004. A goodly feast . . . a cup of mellow wine: feasting in Bronze Age Cyprus. Hesperia 73: 281-300.
Stewart JR, Dikaios P. 1962. The Swedish Cyprus Expedition: The Stone Age and The Early Bronze Age in Cyprus, vol. IV, part 1A. Lund: Swedish Cyprus Expedition.
Swiny S. 1980. Bronze Age gaming stones from Cyprus. Report of the Department of Antiquities, Cyprus 1980: 54-78.
Swiny S. 1986. The Kent State University Expedition to Episkopi Phaneromeni, part 2. Studies in Mediterranean Archaeology 74. Goteborg: Paul Åstroms Förlag.
Swiny S, Rapp G, Herscher E, editors. 2003. Sotira Kaminoudhia: An Early Bronze Age Site in Cyprus. CAARI Monograph Series 4. ASOR Archaeological Reports 8. Boston: American Schools of Oriental Research.
Talalay LE, Cullen T. 2002. Sexual ambiguity in plank figures from Bronze Age Cyprus. In: Bolger D, Serwint, N, editors. Engendering Aphrodite: Women and Society in Ancient Cyprus. pp. 181-195. American Schools of Oriental Research Archaeological Reports 7; Cyprus American Archaeological Research Institute Monograph Series 3. Boston: American Schools of Oriental Research.
Taylor RE, Bar-Yosef O. 2014. Radiocarbon Dating, 2nd ed. Walnut Creek, CA: Left Coast Press.
Urbanus, J. 2024. In the time of the copper kings. Archaeology 77(1): 32-37.

van der Veen, M. 2007. Formation processes of desiccated and carbonized plant remains – the identification of routine practice. Journal of Archaeological Science 34(6): 968-990.
Wang RJ, Al-Saffar SI, Rogers J, Hahn MW. 2023. Human generation times across the past 250,000 years. Science Advances 9(1): Jan 6.
Webb JM, Knapp AB. 2021. Rethinking Middle Bronze Age communities on Cyprus: "egalitarian" and isolated or complex and interconnected? Journal of Archaeological Research 29: 203-253.
Xenophontos C. 1991. Picrolite, its nature, provenance, and possible distribution patterns in the Chalcolithic Period of Cyprus. Bulletin of the American Schools of Oriental Research 282/283: 127-138.